THE REPUTATION OF A CHURCH

The Reputation of a Church

G. Avery Lee

BROADMAN PRESS/NASHVILLE, TENNESSEE

Dewey Decimal Classification Number: 260
Library of Congress Catalog Card Number: 71–128857
Printed in the United States of America
21.5S70KSP

TO
The Congregation of the
SAINT CHARLES AVENUE
BAPTIST CHURCH

Preface

The basic theme of this book is found in chapter 1. Although I am not a historian, historical situations have a fascination and historical novels are exciting. The phrase "history repeats itself" can be seen in every era, and it is discouraging that we do not seem to learn from history. History is not "bunk," as Henry Ford claimed; it is the account of real people in actual situations. We can learn from history, *if we will*. Hopefully, we can profit from this look at some of the historical churches of the New Testament.

In most cases credit has been given to sources from which material has been taken. Historical data about the cities is not documented. I have drawn heavily from *Harper's Bible Dictionary*, edited by Madeline A. and J. Lane Miller. Dr. George Kelm, professor of archaeology at New Orleans Baptist Theological Seminary, says that the data is accurate enough, although scholars vary at some points.

My thanks go to my secretary, Mrs. George (Valerie) Pierce, and to the congregation of the St. Charles Avenue Baptist Church in New Orleans, who patiently listened to these "chapters" when they were sermons. Many personal and local references have been kept with the idea that knowing the locale and background might help a reader look at his own church and city in a similar light.

G. Avery Lee
New Orleans, Louisiana

CONTENTS

CHAPTER ONE

The Reputation of a Church
Ephesians 5:21–33

Writing in a national magazine about her religious experience, a woman said that early in her career she turned from the church because it seemed to her to have too little contact with either the first century or the twentieth to be significant. In other words, she was saying that today's church is both unbiblical and irrelevant. "Surely," she said, "we have the right to expect that the church shall be in contact with reality somewhere."

The implied either/or suggests that it is possible for the church to have contact with either the first or the twentieth century, but not with both. That is, it can be either biblical or relevant, but not both. This is not the case. Biblical authenticity and modern relevance are two sides of the same coin.

Being in touch with the first century is more than merely repeating the words of the first century, making frequent complimentary remarks about it, or trying to act like it. Being concerned about the twentieth century and trying to solve its problems should be more than a desire to be contemporary. Concern is not Christian unless it stems from the conviction that an event which happened in the first century can be understood only in the light of the contemporary scene. That event is what Dr. George Schweitzer calls "the Jesus event" and what the

New Testament calls "The Word became flesh and dwelt among us" (John 1:14, RSV).

In this book we shall take a look at some cities and churches of the New Testament. Our purpose is to provide some contact between the first and twentieth centuries—some historical authenticity and some modern relevance. The conditions of the first century are surprisingly similar to the situations of today.

A sharing of some of the first-century experiences can give us of the twentieth century an idea of the sources of power of those churches and cause us to see that what is presented there in concrete terms still has decided relevance. We possess much in common. Human nature has not changed in these intervening centuries. Their problems were much the same as ours; or, in reverse, most of what confronts us they faced, too. The cast of characters in the drama has changed and the location of the action is different, but the plot remains basically the same. We find ourselves on stage with the spotlight focused on us. But the light will shift between them and us, as a sort of split-level stage effect, so that what is revealed about them will better enable us to play our role in the unfolding drama of Christian faith more effectively.

I have chosen some first-century cities—much as I earlier used some New Testament "roads" [1]—to illustrate the life of the church in those cities as well as to look at ourselves. The environment, culture, and mood of a city can affect a church. In like manner, the attitude, motivation, and approach of a church can rub off on a city.

For many years the United States was a rural nation and people. That has changed. We have become urban, and our life-style has totally changed. As Truman Douglass once bluntly told a conference on rural church life: "We are all people of the city. From the city irradiate the lines of influence which shape the ideas, the tastes, the standards, the folkways, the value judgments, the hopes of the nation. I am not calling upon you to give your approval to this situation. I am suggesting that we must face it as a fact of life." [2]

In one of his writings (I don't know where) Harry Golden, *The Carolina Israelite,* gives us a clue. He imagines Paul going for the first time to a pagan Roman city. Inquiring about the latest Gallup Poll, Paul learns that 63 percent of the people belong to Jupiter; 21 percent to Mithras; 2 percent to Jesus; and 14 percent don't care. Had Paul been a different man, Golden says, he would have packed up and gone home, especially after hearing a taxi driver say: "We ought to hang that bald-headed little Jew!"

But Paul went to those cities, and churches sprang up!

If yesterday's church was weak or strong, what made it that way? If today's church is sick or healthy, why is it that way?

So we begin with "The Reputation of a Church."

Most of us are interested in our reputations. We want them to be good. We want to be well thought of. In one form or another, we have heard the old statement: "Reputation is what people think of us; character is what we actually are." Yet, basically, our reputation is based upon what we do because of our inner character. Many times a reputation has been gained because of past action and continues long after the attributes that brought the reputation have disappeared.

In business, for example, a firm may gain a reputation for producing an outstanding product of high quality. This particular article is automatically identified as the best in its field. People ask for it by name. Then, through management changes, sale of the company, or other factors, the quality slips. It takes some time for the buying public to catch on to the lower quality of the product. But they do catch on, and resistance sets in.

Churches get reputations, too, you know. It is quite possible that a church may enjoy a reputation for warmth, spirituality, evangelism, missions, and efficiency gained through the years. Yet it may have lost entirely those attributes which once gained it renown. On the other hand, a church may be known as cold, indifferent, sophisticated, and formal. Now all that may be changed, but people still look at it in the same old way. You see, reputations are not only hard to come by, they die hard and change slowly.

One reason for looking at these churches of the New Testament is to see that those people were pretty much like us, or we are like them, whichever way you prefer. Their problems were much the same as ours. Their failures and successes were due to the same human and spiritual forces which make for failure or success today. Therefore, we are, in a very real way, talking about ourselves as we take a look at them. We ought thereby to learn better how to be about the business of being a true church.

Now let's take a look at a few characteristics that go to make up the reputation of a church.

For one thing there is *friendliness,* or the welcoming of people to the church. We ought not to fawn over people like a Great Dane puppy, nor should we applaud when the visitors stand. Sometimes an over aggressive friendliness is lacking in the depth of sincerity. Sometimes the fertile imaginations of contrived gimmicks used in welcoming visitors can be anything but friendly. One fellow, commenting on such schemes, made this tongue-in-cheek observation: "My idea is that we provide each visitor with a 'beanie' that has a small red light fastened to its top . . . Every visitor would then be recognized by the flashing red light atop their heads." [3]

What makes friendliness anyway? Obviously, friendly people. But as much as anything "a sense of oneness" is vital. That is, the kind of emotional attitude described by the psalmist, saying: "I was glad when they said unto me, Let us go into the house of the Lord" (Psalm 122:1). Or the way the Christians were described on the day of Pentecost as being together in one place, in one accord.

If we come to the house of the Lord grudgingly, out of a sense of obligation rather than with a sense of joy at being in the Lord's presence, if we come to be seen of men rather than to see God, if we come to criticize instead of to worship, if we are not happy, not sold on our church, and with no feeling of the joy of salvation, then our own unhappiness will rub off on others.

The real responsibility for worship is on the worshiper more than it is on the congregation. Anyone who comes to church should automatically feel welcome, for it is God's house. The burden, the responsibility, the motivation, the reason for being present is laid upon the worshiper. Even so, those of us already present should make worship the kind of experience that every Lord's Day causes the worshiper to rejoice in that day and be glad in it.

A second thing people want to know about a church is *its attitude toward people*. Is it interested in people for their own sake? Does it want the gospel to be heard by all people? Does it restrict its efforts and appeal to some small segment? While it is largely true that like seeks like and kind looks for kind, and there is something about those of kindred mind having much in common, no church ought ever to have the kind of exclusiveness that is associated with a closed membership country club. Before God in worship, all men stand alike.

Some years ago the church emphasis got off on a young people's kick. Such statements as "a young people's church" or "a young people's pastor" were bandied about. All that was good, for it pointed out an obvious neglect. It got some churches back on the track of giving some attention to the spiritual preparation of tomorrow's leadership. But we soon came to realize that no church can exist on any one age emphasis. The church must be for all people, of all ages, of all classes, of all conditions. If there are limitations, let not the church establish them.

One of the most delightful experiences I ever had was to serve as pastor of the University Baptist Church of Champaign, Illinois, adjacent to one of the largest universities in the world. Approximately 85 percent of the membership and 90 percent of the attendance was university students. It was as challenging and stimulating a congregation as a fellow could ever find. But there was something missing, at least for me. I wanted to feel the exuberance of high schoolers, to be with young couples as they began their families and started the upward climb in their professions, to learn from those of the middle years, and to associate with the saints who were gnarled from the struggles of the years.

Today's church "kick" seems to be to get involved in the poverty program, go into the ghetto, and that sort of thing. The church ought to do this, but this isn't all it should do and be.

The church is made up of people, people gathered in the fellowship of belief in Christ, people of all conditions of life. The church is not a social club, although the best of social life is to be found in it. The church is not social action, although it should act within the framework of society. The church is the body of Christ, a fellowship of believers existing for service to man in the name, spirit, and manner of Jesus Christ. The church is the instrument which God has ordained for the proclamation of his redeeming love. As such, it is for all people.

Another facet of a church's reputation is its *courage*. There seems to be a deadly timidity that characterizes too many churches of today. We bring up our big guns and train them on alcoholism, narcotics, gambling, and other such matters, as rightly we should. But we find it decidedly uncomfortable to cut across established class lines, to go counter to cultural patterns, or to take the risk of letting the gospel speak to our manifold social conditions.

Have we lost heart for the task? Have we become too comfortable? Does anyone really expect the church to have anything worthwhile to say? Have we lost confidence in our mission, our sense of being sent to redeem the world?

The church which fears a new position, the church which lurks timidly in the crowd, the church that does not speak with the voice of conscience and authority will be shunted aside by the on-rushing world. The church without courage has no new word to utter because it has no fresh word from God, nor does it seek or expect any new word. Without courage, a church is not the church.

The church will never regain its old power, its old thrill, its old spirit of adventure, its old place of acknowledged leadership until it can face change in the same spirit that science faces change. The principles of Christian faith are eternal, but the expressions of that faith must change and seek new forms.

I'm grateful for the historic courage of this church. I pray that I may in some measure live up to the traditions of this free pulpit so as not to abuse but to bring the real light of the gospel to bear upon our day in both a biblical and a relevant manner.

In this same mood, let me mention a fourth factor in a church's reputation. As a church do we conform to the cultural status quo, or *do we seek to transform our society?* I remember some years ago hearing Dr. Henry Hitt Crane of Detroit. He asked his hearers whether or not they were thermometers, merely registering the social temperature of the day; or whether they were thermostats, controlling the social climate and conditions. This is a question we must ask.

Carlyle Marney says: ". . . the death of religion comes with the death of any high hope of adventure. The moment (our) youngsters feel that nothing truly adventurous or daring or new or truly sacrificial will happen in this place, they go looking for the place where such can be expected."

Marney said that in 1963, and we have seen youth go looking. Then Dr. Marney went on to remind us that the authority of the church comes from God: "We must recover this source of authority. We speak for God in Jesus Christ. If a man or a church becomes convinced in any culture that we must speak for Christ we foreswear social acceptance—for we will speak of things that are not socially acceptable; we forego any insurance of tranquility, for we will be dealing with matters that are turbulent. We foredoom ourselves to isolation; we forsake the established; we foreshorten our peace—when we speak for Christ." [4]

Come along, now, to the most important item in the reputation of a church: *its spiritual life*. Let's not get this confused with how much we pray, or what kind of songs we sing, or how much activity we have.

One test of a church's spirituality is what happens to its people outside the church. And this particularly applies to its youth. A recent book by Fred Heichinger, education editor of the New York *Times,* is called *Teen-Aged Tyranny*. He discusses young people who are not socially or economically underprivileged, rather they are schooled in the most expensive school system any nation ever had, and their material advantages exceed any in history. One sentence stands out in this chronicle of youthful violence and promiscuity: "Since 84 per cent of today's teen-agers are church members and more than half attend church regularly, they could undoubtedly be influenced strongly by religious values." [5]

That youth is not strongly influenced by the church confronts us on every page of this book. Why?

Yet, in the face of that, there is evidence that today's youth does show some influence of the church. We can see it in certain evangelical traditions whose youth goes to Fort Lauderdale each year, or those who went to the 1969 summer music festivals, or those who set up coffeehouse type ministries wherever their fellow youth gathers. We can see it in the Peace Corps or in our own denomination's program of summer missions. We can see it in concerned social action. And who is to say that, despite some of the radicalism, many of the demonstrations have their original motive of idealism coming from some church group. Demonstrators or destroyers? and there is a difference. If we really want to know, let us have our youth speak and then listen, *really listen,* to what they are saying.

Another factor that tests a church's spirituality that is often overlooked, and it is difficult to judge, is what do its members do when they leave one town and move to another place?

Some just find themselves in a new place and will not allow themselves to be weaned away from their previous church love. A few try to transplant their old culture in the new environment. Some want to rest. Others just yearn. They hang their harps on the willows and weep for some remembered Zion. I confess that it bothers me that too many of our people identify with some branch of the Christian family other than Baptist when they leave us. I don't like that, for I'm too selfish to want to lose anyone. But I am glad that most of ours do keep on identifying themselves with Christian faith in some expression.

There are those who come into a new situation and take up as if they had been there always. What a wonderful idea we get from them about the reputation of their former church. How grateful we are for some in this church like that. I wish that some two hundred of our former members who no longer live in New Orleans would show their love for St. Charles by activating themselves in another church and that those who moved to New Orleans would do the same here.

Socrates once said: "The way to gain a good reputation is to try and be what you desire to appear."

A person may be better than his reputation but never better than his principles. The same is true of a church. The reputation of a church depends upon the people who are its members. Part of the making of a reputation depends upon what is said. If a thing is said often enough, whether it is good or bad, people will believe it for a time. Hitler proved that. But reputation rests upon reality. And those who have no reality are soon found out.

Does a good reputation mean that something good is always said? Not necessarily. A person, or a church, is known as much by its enemies as by its friends. There are times when the vocal power of an enemy can do more good than the voices of friends. There are some persons, some groups, some interests that I *want* to be against me and the church. That way we are both identified.

Martin Luther once said: "The church is never in more perilous state than when she has quiet and peace."

If that be true, then today's church stands at the threshold of its most glorious days. Jesus said: "Woe to you, when all men speak well of you, for so their fathers did to the false prophets" (Luke 6:26, RSV).

And again Jesus said: "Blessed are ye, when men shall revile you, and persecute you, and shall say all manner of evil against you falsely, for my sake" (Matt. 5:11).

The reputation of one's personal Christian faith, or of the

truth of the church's Christian witness, looks to yet another statement of Jesus: "By this [truth] shall all men know that ye are my disciples, if ye have love one to another" (John 13:35).

The test is: How much do we love? What is our concern, our compassion?

Does evil give us opposition, or does it ignore us? Not all opposition means that we are in the center of God's will, by any means. Remember, Jesus said we are blessed when we are reviled *for his sake*.

Often, when I hear a person's or a church's reputation questioned or maligned, I think of a story told about Joe DiMaggio, the famed "Yankee Clipper." During a game in the 1941 World Series, DiMaggio went hitless against the pitching of Whitlow Wyatt and was being heckled about it. DiMaggio said: "It wasn't DiMaggio against Wyatt; it was the Yankees against the Dodgers: And the Yankees won!"

So! it's the church against evil, *and the church will win!*

NOTES

1. G. Avery Lee, *Roads to God* (Nashville: Broadman Press, 1969).

2. Everett C. Parker, "Truman Bartlett Douglass: 1901–69." Copyright 1919 Christian Century Foundation. Reprinted by permission from the June 11, 1969 issue of *The Christian Century*.

3. Waddell Waters, *The Baptist Program,* January, 1958, p. 2.

4. Carlyle Marney, "The Recovery of Courage." Copyright 1963 Christian Century Foundation. Reprinted by permission from the December 1963 issue of *The Pulpit*.

5. Quoted in "Youth and the Church," *Christianity Today,* January 3, 1964, p. 20.

CHAPTER TWO:

Jerusalem, Where It All Began

Acts 1:6–9; 2:1–4,41–42

Some time ago a public opinion poll asked a cross-section of Americans to give their impressions about certain United States cities. The cities were to be ranked according to the best-looking women, the best year-round climate, the best food, the most beautiful setting, the gayest night life, the most historical interest, the best place to make a living, and so on. The poll asked nothing about the religious climate of the cities named. But that question *is* important. Is any modern city of our time noted for its atmosphere of godliness?

The city is no new phenomenon, not even the sprawling metropolis. Lewis Mumford's book *The City in History* points this out. Biblical tradition gives us a prolonged view of cities and city-minded men. The earliest cities were contrived; they grew by plan rather than by accident. It is not incidental that the earliest cities were important seats of worship, that they were places where religious concern was important, and that man's place in the stream of life was seriously considered.

It is true that the Christian church was not at first an important part of the life of those cities, for they were founded before Christianity was born. But other religions were vital. Paul recognized the strategic value of the cities, so he planted Christian churches in them.

"The church" or "the New Testament church," whatever those terms may mean, has been the subject for many writers. In more recent times, the doctrine of the church has come in for much consideration. In ecumenical circles, and in the spirit of ecumenism, this is necessary. By and large, we Baptists have ignored the subject. Very little has been written about those early churches which figured so prominently in the inauguration and propagation of Christian faith.

The word *ekklesia,* which we translate *church,* occurs one hundred and fourteen times in the New Testament: three times in Matthew, twenty-three times in Acts, sixty-two times in Paul's Letters, twice in Hebrews, once in James, three times in Third John, and twenty times in Revelation. Among the Hebrews, the *ekklesia* was the assembly of the congregation of Israel before the tabernacle. To the Greeks, the *ekklesia* was the assembly of the citizens of a free city-state. The early Christians used the term to convey the same general idea of the "called out," but to the Christians the assembled ones were those who gathered around the common belief in Jesus Christ as Lord.

There are three general uses of the word *ekklesia* among the early Christians:

1. To denote the institution called the church.

2. To denote a particular congregation, which is the most predominate usage.

3. To refer to all believers in Christ, that is, all who are saved by faith in Jesus Christ.

Jerusalem, where it all began, is where we start. After all, Jerusalem *is* the "mother church." Jesus told his disciples to begin preaching there, and then fan out in an ever-widening circle so that the gospel would reach Judea, Samaria, and the world. And this has been done.

The New Testament does not give us a complete story of

early church history. How we wish it did! We are not told specifically how churches were organized. We do know that the gospel was preached in a given community, men and women believed and accepted Christ as Savior, and then they voluntarily banded together around their common beliefs.

Jerusalem was the first church to be organized, and it was some ten years later that the church at Antioch came into being. Luke dates the beginning of the church at Pentecost, and in one sense he is right. The church had existed prior to Pentecost, but it was somewhat as a child exists before birth—in embryo.

There are many things about this church at Jerusalem which cause Baptists to believe that their concept of the church is very close to that of the New Testament. Some Baptists say closer than that of any other church. However, we should never allow ourselves to fall into the trap of setting uncertain "landmarks" for ourselves while berating "apostolic succession" in others. There is no real value or virtue in maintaining antiquity, unless it has some vitality for today.

There are, however, a few things from Jerusalem which we hold as New Testament convictions concerning the church. Sometimes we Baptists have held these convictions alone; sometimes with others. Dr. E. F. Scott, a scholar who is not a Baptist, has an article in *The Interpreter's Bible* which describes some of these things which we are inclined to call Baptist distinctives.

For one thing, there was no creed which all must accept. This was a fellowship which accepted no authority but that of the Spirit, so there was no fixed statement of belief. That came much later. There were certain things held as primary convictions on which the followers of Jesus agreed, and it was this common faith which brought them together. Among those beliefs were:

Acknowledgment of Jesus as Messiah, or Savior;

Agreement that Jesus' teachings were the rule of life;

Assurance of Jesus' resurrection;

Belief that Jesus would return to earth to establish the kingdom of God on earth and that he would return soon;

Belief in Jesus' death as the means by which both personal salvation and the Kingdom were made possible.

In the second place, among this group there was great freedom of interpretation. These convictions were not defined in rigid terms. Each believer was left free to interpret in his own way as he felt directed by the Spirit of God. And, from the first, there were differences of opinion and interpretation. All that was required was the heartfelt response to Jesus and his message, and no restraint was laid on the faculties of reason which might present the same truth in different ways to different men.

For the most part, Baptists have followed this principle. However, there have always been some Baptists who would restrict others and try to make them conform. This is true among Southern Baptists today. Fellowship is withdrawn from Baptist churches who have differing ideas about baptism and the Lord's Supper. Even the past president of the Southern Baptist Convention, Dr. W. A. Criswell, would insist that all who do not subscribe in full to "Statements of Faith" should get out. This, despite our heritage.

A third thing about the Jerusalem church was that they had two ordinances, neither of which had anything to do with salvation but both of which were symbolic of what had already been done: baptism, which was external evidence that the believer had already committed himself to Christ and had entered a new way of life, and the Lord's Supper, which was continued as a memorial to show the significance of Jesus' death.

Now, let's take a close look at the Jerusalem church and

consider its membership. At first, it was entirely Jewish. The first members were Jews. The first preachers were Jews. Christianity is the proper outcome and fulfilment of Judaism. It links the fundamental ideas of the Old Testament: God, sin, and promised redemption, with Jesus Christ as the Messiah who fulfilled the promises of God.

That God intended that the Gentiles should share in the gospel was hard for the Jewish congregation of the Jerusalem church to learn. There was precedent in the Old Testament where Jonah preached to Nineveh about the universality of God's salvation. Even after Peter's experience with Cornelius, the members of the church in Jerusalem could not see the fulness of the doctrine of missionary expansion.

It is at this point that we see a serious defect in this church, a defect which led them into gradual decline. It is tragic for any group of Christians when they begin to slack off in their expansion of the gospel. It is not giving which hurts a church. Rather, it is when a church keeps to itself what must be shared that the church suffers.

The growth of the Jerusalem church was at first very rapid—from the one hundred and twenty in the upper room, to the three thousand on the day of Pentecost and the five thousand recorded in Acts 4:4. Then we have no more record. Only the episode of the dispute with the Antioch church.

There is another thing for us to see: the significance and lasting value of the church at Jerusalem. Their brief career has been commonly treated as a mere prelude to the real history of the expansion of Christianity which began with Paul's missionary journeys to the Gentile world. But there are some truly significant things which Christians of the world owe to this church.

First, the Jerusalem church saved Christianity. With the death of Jesus his cause seemed doomed to failure. But following the resurrection, this handful of believers kept Christianity alive. They did more than preserve; they founded a society unique in character. They existed under earthly conditions, but they stood by heavenly convictions. They gave us that which is vital to the perpetuation of the Christian faith: believer's baptism, a symbolic Lord's Supper, and lives of charity and chastity.

In the second place, though the church remained secluded and fell into the background with the advent of Paul, it continued to make its presence felt. It provided the base of operations for the larger work. In fact, Luke thinks of each missionary expedition as setting out from Jerusalem and returning there. All the other churches looked to Jerusalem for guidance, for it served as a check and balance to help those other churches who had little or no Old Testament roots and background. The new churches were thus enabled to get firmly anchored in the basic beliefs about God, sin, promised redemption, and Christ as Savior.

Finally, in a positive, definite way, this elder church made its priceless contribution. It brought together and preserved for all time those records of the life and teachings of Jesus which we know as the four Gospels.

Although the church was conservative, perhaps even a bit reactionary, and was slow to expand in the meeting of new occasions and new responsibilities, it kept alive the significance of Jesus' life and teachings. This is the chief value of conservatism. We need the conservatives to hold on to the past and keep alive that which is good. But we also need the progressives to adapt the old and fit it to changing conditions and situations. It is sad that there is so much conflict between these two needed positions.

It is a misfortune that this church left no records or documents of its own that are comparable to the book of Acts or the epistles of Paul. But we do know that, on the whole, they maintained a faithful witness to Jesus Christ. They treasured the memory of Christ. Their hope was fixed on the kind of society Jesus talked about. If the church in Jerusalem took little part in the expansion, at least it guarded the message upon which Christians ever since have depended.

Paul was ever mindful of his debt to the Jerusalem church. He indignantly denied that he preached any gospel other than what they preached, though there were differences of interpretation. Said Paul: "Whether it were I or they, so we preach, and so ye believed" (1 Cor. 15:11).

CHAPTER THREE:

Philippi, in the Secular City

Acts 16:11–15

The pattern of "capturing the cities for Christ" is seen once again as we consider the church at Philippi. It is fortunate that Paul wrote this tenderest of all his epistles, for it enables us to know quite a bit more about this church than some of the others in the New Testament.

Philippi, the first European city to be touched by the Christian faith, was truly a secular city. It was on the great Roman road between the Adriatic Sea and the Hellespont. Krenidas was its original name, a name derived from the many springs of water in the area. Phillip of Macedon, the father of Alexander the Great, learned that gold had been discovered in the adjoining mountains, and he wanted that gold, so he captured the area and renamed it after himself. Philippi became a Roman province some 150 years before Christ.

In the year 42 B.C. a decisive battle was fought in the plains of Philippi. The forces of Brutus and Cassius met the troops of Octavious Augustus and Marc Antony. In the first battle Cassius committed suicide; in the second Brutus did the same. Octavious was victor and he established a military colony in Philippi that remained as a major Roman domicile for centuries thereafter.

In addition, Philippi was a religious and philosophical center.

Aristotle had been there, and the chief shrine for the worship of Dionysis was located in the nearby mountain of Pangaeus.

So, once again we see a sophisticated, cultured, cosmopolitan, strategic city being invaded by a small group of Christians in an effort to plant their faith. While Philippi is referred to as the chief city of the district, we sometimes get the feeling that there is a faint odor of chamber of commerce-like pride in itself (which every city, ours included, ought to have).

Paul was drawn to Philippi in the course of what we call the second missionary journey. Roadblocks seemed to get in his way as he tried time and again to turn to other centers of population. Twice he says the Holy Spirit prevented him from further preaching in Asia. Perhaps he was already hearing the call and responding to the challenge of Europe. After all, Rome was in Europe, and Rome was the capital of the world. Anyway, at Troas Paul had the vision of the man calling, "Come over to Macedonia and help us" (Acts 16:9, RSV).

Paul was always obedient to what he called "the heavenly vision;" so, taking this as a sign from heaven, he sailed straight-way for Europe. Silas was with him from Antioch. Timothy joined him at Lystra, and Luke at Troy. This is the first personal appearance of Luke in the Acts narrative. Here were four Christian missionaries crossing from the Orient to the Occident to proclaim the good news that "God was in Christ reconciling the world." Xerxes' crossing the Hellespont to conquer Greece; Hannibal's scaling the Alps to conquer Italy; and Caesar's crossing the Rubicon were not so momentous events in history as Paul's crossing into Europe with the gospel.

When Paul turned westward to Europe, the course of human history from that day to this was established with Christianity expanding toward Europe and eventually to us. Had Paul not gone to Europe, the entire course of history would have been different: For better or for worse, who knows? But imagine the difference if the heavenly vision had called him eastward! The gospel light would have shone on the Orient instead of on Europe, England, and the United States.

Some scholars have suggested that Luke had been planting seed in Paul's mind that was responsible for the vision. Well, the seed of the gospel can be planted in many ways. If this view is correct, then we of the Western world owe Luke an even greater debt. The suggestion is that Philippi may have been Luke's hometown and he was anxious for them to know this good news which he had found so personally satisfying. Thus, the reason for Luke's referring to ". . . the chief city in this district." It would also explain some of Luke's familiarity with some of the details of the city, particularly his knowledge of the small group who met by the riverside for worship.

A little more than a mile west of the city was the river Gangas. Judaism was too small to have a synagogue in the city. The men had lost faith and no longer worshiped, but the women kept their worship in a place near the river. Hence, Luke records the first event of importance: "On the sabbath day we went outside the gate to the riverside, where we supposed there was a place of prayer; and we sat down and spoke to the women who had come together. One who heard us was a woman named Lydia. . . . The Lord opened her heart to give heed to what was said by Paul. And when she was baptized, with her household, she besought us, saying, . . . 'Come to my house and stay'" (Acts 16:13–15, RSV).

There is a second event that marks the early influence of Paul in Philippi. Because Paul rebuked the exploitation of a girl who was being used as a fortune-teller and thus interfered with the profit being made by a group of unscrupulous men, he and Silas were arrested and placed in prison.

How strange it is that when the gospel is brought to bear on the degradation of human beings so that it interferes with the making of money it runs into trouble. "Just stick to the simple gospel," say such folk, "and leave off these social applications." Well, we are in good company with Paul and Silas whenever we try to apply the Christian faith to daily life, especially where there is some exploitation and degradation of human beings.

While Paul and Silas were in prison, there was a dramatic earthquake which resulted in the conversion of the jailer. " 'Men, what must I do to be saved?' And they said, 'Believe in the Lord Jesus, and you will be saved.' . . . And they spoke the word of the Lord to him and to all that were in his house. . . . And he was baptized at once, with all his family" (Acts 16:30–33, RSV).

This was Paul's first experience in prison. It was not to be his last. Nor was this the last imprisonment of Christians, for through the centuries Christians have been placed in jail, even in America.

In Chesterfield, Virginia, in the late 1700's, John Weatherford was placed in prison. The jailer, a rather kind-hearted man, allowed the prisoner some privileges. There were complaints, so the sheriff was ordered to confine "said Weatherford strictly to his cell." But Weatherford preached through the bars. His hands were cut with whips and knives, so he sprinkled his blood on the people in expressive gestures.

Nearly a century later, a Dr. Hatcher, who was then the president of Richmond College, was on a fund-raising tour. In a country church the pastor said: "Dr. Hatcher, I want my people to do nobly but I fear they will not. Our richest member is our stingiest member. Ten dollars is his maximum contribution to any object. Our members are kept from doing their duty by waiting for him to lead."

Dr. Hatcher told the story of how Virginia Baptists had struggled for religious freedom. He told the story of John Weatherford, then he appealed for funds. That wealthy man arose to speak, saying: "Dr. Hatcher, when I was a small boy my father took me to the funeral of Parson Weatherford at the country burying ground in Pittslyvania. As was the custom in those days and at that place the people passed by the open casket and viewed the remains. I was too small to look in the casket and my father lifted me up so I could see. Parson Weatherford's hands were folded across his pulseless bosom. They were scarred with white marks. Those white marks were stamped indelibly on my young mind. I have thought about them a thousand times and wondered what caused them. You have explained it tonight. I will give five hundred dollars to endow a college of a denomination which produces men like Parson Weatherford."

From these three incidents—the riverside preaching with the conversion of Lydia; the episode with the girl that resulted in prison, and the conversion of the jailer—came the development of an impressive Christian community in the secular city of Philippi. We shall return to these episodes a bit later, but right now let us consider some lessons we can learn from the church at Philippi.

For one thing, note the prominence of women. Macedonia was one place in the ancient world where women held an honored position even before Christianity came along. Ancient inscriptions found there commonly record the mother's name instead of the father's. Add to this the dignity which Christ conferred upon women, and we have the New Testament church in which women ranked the highest.

The church in Philippi got its start as the result of a women's prayer meeting, remember. Its first convert was a business-woman named Lydia. She later carried the gospel to her home in Thyatira and was responsible for starting one of the seven churches of Asia.

Such a process continues to be effective. Several years ago Mrs. Oscar McMillan moved from our area to Hahnville, Louisiana, on the west bank of the Mississippi River. There was no Baptist church there, so Ethel kept her membership with us. She attended the Luling Baptist Church and divided her tithe between them and us. In 1966 she and a neighbor began a prayer meeting whose main object of prayer was to have a Baptist church in Hahnville. A few months later a New Orleans Baptist Theological Seminary student appeared on the scene there. To make the story short, everything seemed to fit in place. The time was right with a prepared readiness. People began to meet in a home. Plans for a church were discussed. Offerings were taken. And in the fall of 1966 a church was organized, and Oscar and Ethel McMillan became charter members. She did not want to sever her long and close ties with our church. But as she and I talked, it was my recommendation that she do so in order to be a charter member of a church for which she had dreamed, prayed, and worked for so many years.

Were it not for the women, many of our churches would be far weaker than they are. Our foreign mission program has become great, financially speaking, largely because of the some fifteen million dollars that come annually from the Lottie Moon Christmas Offering for missions. *Approximately 60 percent of all our foreign missionaries in service today are women!*

A second thing about this church was its contagious spirit of joy. In Paul's letter to them the note of joy is a recurring theme, like the beautiful melody of a Tchaikovsky symphony. One reason for the rejoicing is found in the phrase, Your fellowship with me in the furtherance of the gospel. So Paul says: "I thank my God for every remembrance of you."

But even in the joy there was cause for sorrow. There was opposition to the church, especially from the pagan Gentiles. There was even some dissension within the group itself. Two of the women, Euodia and Syntyche, had a difference of opinion. And church squabbles are always sad occasions. Christianity should produce happiness. It should bring a sense of personal peace with God, a feeling of goodwill towards one's fellowman, and a means of victory over adversity. Some lines from Robert Burns tell us:

> "It's no' in title nor in rank,
> It's no' in wealth like Lon'on bank,
>   To purchase peace and rest.
> If happiness cannot have her seat
>   And center in the breast,
> We may be wise, or rich, or great,
>   But never can be blest."

Happiness is an attitude toward life. Outward circumstances, in themselves, can neither give nor destroy happiness. Jesus taught us in the Beatitudes that happiness in life depends upon character, not circumstances. Those Christians in Philippi lived in a hostile and depressing environment, yet they were joyful. If we honestly believe that to them that love God, all things work together for good, then we can understand Paul's "Rejoice in the Lord always; again I will say, Rejoice" (Phil. 4:4, RSV).

Philippi is a shining example of a church that is liberal in its stewardship. There are four ways for us to see this.

First, the liberality of the poor: "Their deep poverty

abounded to the riches of their liberality." It is almost an axiom of truth that poor people are proportionately more generous than the wealthy. One wealthy man once said, "I can give $10,000 and never eat a biscuit less for breakfast." You see, it is hard for a wealthy person to make a sacrifice. It is the less affluent who give sacrificially. And those Philippians gave beyond their ability. They sacrificed.

Second, their gifts were unsolicited. That is, they gave "of their own accord." They saw need and opportunity, and they acted. There are always folk who anticipate and send a contribution before it is asked for. And sometimes there are those whose giving is larger than even the pastor would have suggested. May their tribe increase!

In the third place, theirs was an insistent liberality: "Beseeching of us the grace and participation in the ministering of the saints." They wanted to give and share. They asked Paul to let them be a part of his labors.

And, fourth, their giving was continuous, not just a one-shot affair. They supported Paul in other places, even in Rome. Money for charity in Jerusalem and for missions in Europe kept coming from this church. They took the initiative. Listen to Paul: "In the beginning of the gospel, when I went forth from Macedonia, no church communicated with me in the way of giving and receiving, but you only. In Thessalonica you sent once and again to my need" (Phil. 4:15–16, author's translation).

Such a spirit of liberal giving is to be desired in any church. Today we far surpass them in possessions, but not always in achievement. Yet, I think that our church has been a lot like Philippi in this respect, and none of us have hurt ourselves in it.

But there was one unfortunate thing about the church in Philippi to which I have already referred. There was a contro-

versy in the church. It is never good for a church to get into
disagreements. Of all people, Christians ought to set the example of being able to live harmoniously with differences of opinion.

Just what the trouble was at Philippi is hard to discover, but it
seems to have centered around two things.

First, the dispute between Euodia and Syntyche. And we do
not know what this was about. They did get it settled, however.
And good thing that they did, for such disputes never accom-
plish anything other than harm for a church and to the cause of
Christ.

In my home church in Oklahoma City, two men got involved
in a dispute. Childhood friends from Arkansas, business asso-
ciates, and fellow deacons, they became bitter enemies. I shall
never forget the stormy church meeting where the fellowship of
the church was withdrawn from one of those men. Then each
began to carry a gun to shoot the other on sight. But neither did
shoot. I was caught in the middle. One of those men paid my
room and board for my freshman year of college, and my
roommate was the son of the other man. That church, to this
day, has never fully recovered from that dispute, although that
was more than three decades ago.

Second, there was evidently some kind of a doctrinal dispute
which included some of the same legalistic insistence we saw
between Jerusalem and Antioch. There are always some who
want to be "guardians of the faith," but they insist that everything must center around *their* interpretation of what the faith is.
To them, everyone else is wrong.

Despite our insistence on the absence of creeds and our
heritage of freedom of interpretation, we Baptists have always
been plagued by this. We still are. Since the second Vatican
Council we have seen internal fusses within the Roman Church

come out into the open. In the meeting in Rome about "collegiality," Pope Paul VI let it be known that *he* is the sole ruler of that Church. And other denominations have the same problems.

Evidently, in Philippi there was some insistence on the part of some of the Jewish Christians that all Gentile converts should be circumcised. Paul had pointed out that he himself was "a Hebrew of the Hebrews," but all that was unnecessary for one to be a Christian.

On the other hand, some of the Gentile Christians seemed to want to discard everything connected with the Old Testament and even adopt some of the pagan practices. And a good bit of the Greek religions has crept into Christian doctrine and practice. The advice of Paul was for them to be sensible and not lose sight of the object of their faith, Jesus Christ!

Come further, now, and see some lessons we can learn from Philippi, not only from these four characteristics but more especially from the conversion of two people: Lydia and the jailer. The major lesson for us to learn is this: solidarity within the church. Remember, when Lydia was converted, so was her household and her home became headquarters for the church. Likewise, when the jailer was converted and baptized, so was his entire household.

God uses various ways to awaken people to their need. Lydia had found something in Judaism that aroused her spiritual sensitivity and made her receptive to Paul's preaching. In the case of the jailer it was an earthquake and a threatened prison break that turned him to God. So the man was led to a consciousness of the need of God in his life.

God does send earthquakes sometimes, not always the shaking of the earth, but the shaking of the foundations of life. He makes life quiver and shake. Losses come, bereavement hits, the bottom falls out, and we are compelled to think of the serious matters of life which we have either neglected or disregarded.

God often places judgment and eternity in full view of our eyes so that we may see the solemn realities of life. Thus the writer of Ecclesiastes can say: "God has made it so, in order that man should fear before him" (Eccl. 3:14, RSV).

The first thing a person awakened by God, however the awakening comes, has to consider is how can he come into the right relationship with God. In other words, it is the jailer's question: "What must I do to be saved? How can sin be forgiven?"

The answer Paul gave is the answer that must be given to any honest seeker. The earnest seeker after God's salvation must be directed away from externals and pointed to the divine Savior in whom he can confidently believe. Jesus Christ is that Savior.

This belief in Jesus Christ is to be followed by an open profession of faith and an active discipleship. Both Lydia and the jailer showed their sincerity, despite not having all of the answers, by believing and being baptized, by winning their families, by wanting to learn more of Christ, and by actively participating in meeting the needs of the Christian community everywhere.

The kingdom of God is like seed sown in the ground. When it takes root in *one life,* great are the results. The conversion of Lydia, the first known convert in Europe, and that of the jailer were the beginnings of an outstanding church whose reputation still lives.

CHAPTER FOUR:

Thessalonica, Expectancy!

Acts 17:1–9; 1 Thessalonians 1

God plants his churches everywhere whether we take part in the planting or not. Often our negligence slows the progress of Christian expansion. Often our resistance to change makes the work more difficult. But God has a way, or ways, of getting his message to people. Thus, when the Jerusalem church was slow, Antioch came along to push the cause of expansion. When the Jewish people resisted the change, the gospel was taken to the Gentiles, beginning at Antioch.

After preaching in Philippi, Paul left Luke there and took Silas with him and journeyed some one hundred miles to Thessalonica, where the second Christian community was established in Europe. There were smaller cities, such as Amphipolis and Apollonia through which he passed, but these smaller places could be evangelized later by Christians from the larger cities. It was Paul's practice to plant churches in large, metropolitan areas, the centers of population and influence, and then radiate from them into the surrounding areas.

Such a procedure is in vogue today as Southern Baptists have expanded to all fifty states. We can understand some of the concern of our brethren in the American Baptist Convention, for they consider such tactics as being more of an invasion than an expansion. I can agree with them when we go into places where there are already established Baptist churches. But it's a bit different in cities where there is no Baptist church at all. For example, when the Manhattan Baptist Church was established in New York, it was the first new Protestant church to be established in New York in some fifty years—almost a half century. That church then became the focal point from which other missions were established within the metropolitan area and even as far away as New Jersey and New England. Today there is a Southern Baptist Convention of churches in New York state.

Thessalonica was already an ancient city when Paul reached it. It was a seaport city built in the shape of an amphitheater, perhaps somewhat similar to our own Crescent City. Not only was it the capitol of Macedonia, it was also the largest city. Renowned for its hot springs, its earlier name was Therme. Cassandra, who inherited one-third of Alexander the Great's empire, was married to Alexander's sister, Thessalonia; so he renamed the city after her. (Those Greeks do a lot for the women they marry!) Rome conquered Macedonia and divided it into four districts, with Thessalonica the capital of one area. Later all four were combined, and Thessalonica was made the capital. In the year 42 B.C. Augustus made it a free city, governed by men of its own selection.

In the time of Paul, Thessalonica was a populous, thriving city, inhabited by Greeks with a mixture of Romans. Many Jews had also come there because of the commercial opportunities. It is one of the few ancient cities to retain some modern importance. In the days of World War I it had a new prominence as the Allies chose it to be their major base of operation against Turkey in that area. Today it is strategically valuable to modern Greece and can be located on maps by the name of Salonika.

The gospel was brought to this city during the course of Paul's second missionary journey. His work in Macedonia radiated from three centers: Philippi, Thessalonica, and Berea. Not only were these strategic cities, but each had a large Jewish colony. Although Paul was chosen as the apostle to the Gentiles, he always went "to the Jews first." He always gave the Jews the first chance to hear and respond to the gospel. But there was a second reason for going to the synagogues. There were many Greeks and Romans who were in various stages of passing from paganism to Judaism, and thus were ready for the fulfilment that is to be found in Jesus Christ.

The chief synagogue of Macedonia was in Thessalonica. Philippi did not have one, remember, so Paul went to the synagogue to preach. The Scripture says that he preached there three sabbaths, but the indication is that he stayed longer than three weeks. Anyway, he preached that Jesus of Nazareth was the fulfilment of Old Testament prophecies concerning the Messiah. One short sentence packs in the results of his ministry: "Some of them were persuaded, and joined Paul and Silas; as did a great many of the devout Greeks and not a few leading women" (Acts 17:4, RSV).

Although the Jews were numerous, it is evident from the two letters that Paul wrote to this church that it was composed largely of Gentiles.

We have a special interest in this church because it received the first letter that Paul wrote. And this first epistle to Thessalonica is probably the oldest Christian document we possess. Older than any other New Testament writing, it has a vital bearing on some of the history and problems of early Christianity. And we still face some of the same issues Paul wrote about nineteen centuries ago.

This community of believers had been Christian but a brief time. They had heard only the simplest of gospel truths. They were not ready for "heavy theology," and they found it difficult to grasp the moral and ethical teachings of Christianity. They needed instruction and training in the foundations of Christian faith. This is a matter we confront, for despite our centuries of advantage, we need instruction in Christian faith and practice.

Paul commended this church first for its possession of Christian graces and second for its evangelistic and missionary zeal. Then, he had some sharp words of warning as well.

Let's look at the warnings first. Chapter 5, verse 14 of the first epistle tells something of the difficulty: "We exhort you, brethren, admonish the idle, encourage the fainthearted, help the weak, be patient with them all" (RSV). In this verse we see three groups of people who were problems of concern. Their counterparts are in every church today.

First, there were the *idle,* sometimes referred to as the disorderly. Dr. James Sullivan of our Sunday School Board, has an old Mississippi phrase which I like. He calls such persons "post whittlers," those old cronies who sit around the town square and whittle down everything—every post, every person, every idea in sight.

Some of those idle ones believed that the end of the world was so close at hand and that Jesus would immediately return that they had no inclination to work. (We shall return to this return-of-Christ idea a bit later on.) Their idleness laid an unnecessarily heavy burden on their brethren and exposed the entire group of Christians to words of reproach from the non-Christians in the city. Paul's letters told them to get busy, get to work, and prove themselves worthy examples of what Christians ought to be: "But we exhort you, brethren, to do so more and more, to aspire to live quietly, to mind your own affairs, and to work with your hands, as we charged you; so that you may command the respect of outsiders, and be dependent on nobody" (1 Thess. 4:10–12, RSV).

Our church, like all others, has its share of those who do not carry their portion of the load. Ours are not loafing around waiting for the return of Christ. Far from that! But we do have too many who are idle.

I often wonder how such people can remain idle in the face of the strict demands of being a follower of Christ or in hearing appeal after appeal to come over to some Macedonia and help. I wonder what being a Christian really means to them, if anything. Perhaps it is because too many follow at such a distance, if they follow at all, that they cannot see the demands or hear the appeals.

A second group was the fainthearted. These were the ones who were disturbed over a point concerning the fate of those who had died. Their question seemed to be: "When the Lord comes back to earth, will those deceased ones be with Christ, or only those who are still alive when he returns?"

There are always those folk who get so bothered about some minor doctrinal or scriptural detail that they will quibble away all of their time on something altogether unimportant and neglect important matters which are obvious.

In that day, and in that church, there was a great deal of confusion over the doctrine of Christ's return. Paul himself was responsible for this, for in his first letter he stated that the return of Christ was at hand.

Any extreme position on this issue will always cause confusion. More important than when will Christ return is whether or not we have made the right decision in faith about his first coming and are thus ready for any return, whenever it may occur. The major message of the New Testament is that sinners need to repent and accept Christ as the Savior, not some marginal matter about when he will return. What difference does it make about a second coming if we are not in right relationship to the first coming?

Paul had to write a second letter in an effort to straighten out the kinks and try to undo some of the damage he had caused.

"Now concerning the coming of our Lord Jesus Christ and our assembling to meet him, we beg you, brethren, not to be quickly shaken in mind or excited, either by spirit or by word, or by letter purporting to be from us, to the effect that the day of the Lord has come" (2 Thess. 2:1–12, RSV).

That the Lord would return, Paul was certain. But as to the time, he was unsure, and certainly it was not for them, or anyone else, to try and determine the exact hour. The business of the Christian is to do the work of the Lord—*spread the gospel!*

The third warning is addressed to the *weak:* not so much weak in faith as in conduct. A problem peculiarly trying to a man of Paul's sensitivities, with his ingrained Hebrew horror of sexual impurity, was the indifference with which many of the Gentile Christians regarded this matter. Paul was always taking them to task for sexual irregularities.

But, before we are too hard on them, let us remember their background. The lessons of Christian purity, based on the Jewish law, were hard for them to learn and understand because the standards were so different from all they had ever practiced even in religious observances. The standards and practices of the Gentiles were far less strict than those of the Jews.

And some among us, with nineteen centuries of background, have not learned very well either. The morals of our present-day sexual practices are pretty loose and getting more so. Sexual immorality, promiscuity, and the like are more prevalent in the United States, Sweden, and other European countries where Christianity has flourished than in any other section of the world, including the Communist world. Hence, all the more reason for those of Thessalonica, and us in New Orleans, to listen to Paul: "For this is the will of God, your sanctification [consecration]: that you abstain from immorality" (1 Thess. 4:3, RSV).

Like most of the other New Testament churches, Thessalonica suffered persecution. In this case, most of it came from the Jews rather than from the pagan Gentiles. Paul's success aroused Jewish jealousy, so a mob was incited to violence. And a mob is never a pretty sight.

The house of Jason, a Jew of property who had been converted, was attacked. Failing to find Paul and Silas, the mob dragged Jason and some other Christians before the authorities. The charges were similar to those brought against Jesus:

Sedition—"They have raised a tumult through the empire."

Treason—"They have set Caesar's authority at defiance, declaring there is another emperor, one called Jesus."

Roman law was fair, however, and Christianity had some protection and security. Jason was put under bond, while Paul and Silas were sent to Berea.

We can understand why the members of the synagogue resented Paul's success. After all, he took some of their members! And Jason was a wealthy member. We do not like to lose members, either, especially active members who work and contribute. But sometimes we do lose. No one likes a proselyter, be he a Baptist or otherwise. We want other people and other churches to leave our members alone. We have some modern proselyters among us. Some are very open about it, and we don't like it. There are far too many people who are not Christian for any of us to resort to sheep stealing. Why, in some cities the competition for members is worse than a fraternity rush or recruiting a good quarterback. It got so bad in one place that the Scripture was paraphrased: "There is more rejoicing over one Baptist who moves his membership than over a sinner who is converted."

One man called me not long ago asking that I extend an invitation to this congregation to come to his church and hear a guest speaker. He said, "Do you believe in twentieth century miracles?"

To which I replied, "Yes, I've seen some."

Taken aback, the man went on: "Well, if your people come and sign a visitor's card, we won't even visit them." My answer to that was: "*That* would be a miracle!"

Paul was unable to visit these young churches as often as he desired; so he wrote letters to them. Twice he wrote to Thessalonica, probably from Corinth. He did visit Macedonia again on his third missionary journey, but that was several years after the letters were written. We can see something of the character of the church and find adequate data by comparing Acts 17:1–9 with both of Paul's letters to the church.

For one thing, the church was born in a revival. Paul's most successful preaching was done there. What he said was received as the Word of the Lord. Paul spoke of their receptivity to the truth and how they turned from idols to serve the Lord, the true and living God. Revivals still result in churches, sometimes.

A second characteristic of the church was what someone has called "the trinity of graces." Said Paul: "We give thanks to God always for you all, constantly mentioning you in our prayers, remembering before our God and Father your work of faith and labor of love and steadfastness of hope in our Lord Jesus Christ" (1 Thess. 1:2–3, RSV).

Now, let's look at that trinity of graces.

First, "your work of faith." Faith worked; it did not sit around in idleness. In the eleventh chapter of Hebrews we read of special deeds in the lives of people which were produced by faith. But the work of faith, in its totality, is the kind of life that is lived before the eyes of people. It is not just deeds done, but the kind of life that produces the deeds. It is not just verbal expression of faith, but visible demonstration. It is not faith or work; it is faith *and* work. And Paul is certainly in full accord with James at this point.

The one who believes that he is here to carry out divine instructions, that there is a coming judgment which will show a person what he has done with his life—such a person will surely produce a different and better kind of life than the person who has no such belief. The life of a Christian should produce the works of faith, and this was being done at Thessalonica.

The second grace was "your labor of love." We are not merely to wish others well and rejoice when good comes to them. That implies no effort on our part. We are to put forth effort in behalf of the sinful, the oppressed, the poor, the sick, the ignorant and see to it that they have help. All this is to be a labor of love in the spirit of Christ, not a begrudging obligation we have to perform. If we do not labor in love, we have not been apt pupils in the school of Christian instruction.

And, third, "your steadfastness of hope." Hope was a characteristic of Thessalonica. In the dark days of their persecution, hope was kept alive by their vivid expectation of the return of Christ. So eager were they in that expectation that they began to get a bit impatient at the delay. It is hope that sustains us in any kind of difficulty: In illness, we hope for health; in battle, we hope for victory; in war, we hope for peace; in distress, we hope for comfort; in sin, we hope for redemption—or we should!

A third characteristic of this church was its vivid belief in the second coming of Christ. It has been said that the Bible can be divided into three sections:

Someone will come. Someone has come. Someone will come again.

For four thousand years the Jews had looked for the coming of the Messiah. That hope was fulfilled in Jesus Christ. Since Jesus left, Christians, and others, have looked for his return. Even the Moslem Mosque of Omayad in the city of Damascus has what is called "the minaret of Christ's return." Tradition says that when Christ does come back, it will be at that spot.

Paul's two letters to Thessalonica contain more about the second coming of Christ than any other sources in the New Testament. There are nine distinct references: 1 Thessalonians 1:10; 2:19; 3:13; 4:14 ff; 5:2; 5:23; 2 Thessalonians 1:7; 2:1; 2:8. By taking these references as a whole, we may see several things.

Paul taught the second coming of Christ so emphatically that the people erroneously believed he would come in their own day. But the time of Christ's return is unknown. There is talk of certain events that will precede his coming, and every age of history has had those same signs that could be and have been interpreted to that end.

In the Pentecostal tradition, in which I grew up, there was a steady diet of what is called premillennialism, that is, those who expect the immediate return of Christ. The "signs of the time" were read and reread each time they changed so as to fit their own interpretation. The books of Daniel in the Old Testament and Revelation in the New Testament were carefully charted and timetables were presented. I've gone to bed many nights as a youngster fearing that come morning when I turned on the water faucet blood would flow out instead of water. There was also the fear that some of the family would be taken during the night—probably my grandmother, since my grandfather was not a professing Christian at that time. All this did for me as a lad was to make me afraid of God and not very happy with him. Then, as I grew older and none of those predictions came to pass, I became skeptical of the whole thing.

I have read a lot and listened to many, and I am unable to come up with any satisfactory answer. I am not much concerned with the second coming of Christ. It does not bother me in the least if there is a visible, bodily return a thousand years before or a thousand years after anything. It may even be that this return of Christ is what he said about "another Comforter." Of this I am sure: We know that Jesus did come. We know the teaching about sin and the necessity of repentance and faith. And unless we have accepted Jesus Christ as Savior and Lord of life as a result of his coming, we are in one whale of a mess whatever second coming there may be.

A final characteristic of the church that receives Paul's enthusiastic commendation is its evangelistic, missionary zeal. These two ought to be parts of the same thing but are not always. Paul said: "For not only has the word of the Lord sounded forth from you in Macedonia and Achaia, but your faith in God has gone forth everywhere" (1 Thess. 1:8, RSV).

Within a brief period of little more than half a century, the Christian community had gone from one church in Jerusalem to a host of churches scattered throughout the Roman Empire, both in Asia and Europe. It has been estimated that by the end of the first century there were some five hundred thousand Christians in the world. Persecution caused some scattering, but evangelistic concern and missionary zeal was responsible for more.

That estimate may be high, for there is no way for us to know from a religious census. But it was the evangelistic-missionary efforts of churches such as Antioch, Philippi, and Thessalonica that produced the change. We do know that in some three hundred years Christianity was the official religion of the Empire, though we are not very happy about how that came to be. As we stop at Thessalonica, remember it was but the year A.D. 52, Christianity was just beginning its march. Only a few consecrated people, plus a lot of others like us—willing but weak in faith and effort—did the work. But from such people came the expansion of the Christian faith to the point where it is now preached on every continent to every people in the world. And, even so, many have never heard, including some who live here in New Orleans.

Even after two thousand years, Christianity is young as religions of the world go. But when churches and individual Christians with an enthusiastic witness to their Christian faith meet their opportunities, people listen and respond. The twentieth century has seen the greatest expansion of Christian faith of all time. However, that expansion has slowed down. The birthrate population explosion is causing us to lose ground. A rising missionary fervor on the part of Islam and Buddhism is taking its toll. Yet, we have the finest opportunity to spread the gospel in all history. Our transportation is better, our communications are better, and our resources are greater. We need wisdom, vision, courage, and consecration to meet the responsibilities and opportunities of our day in the same manner that those early Christians met theirs.

CHAPTER FIVE

Ephesus, the Materialistic Mood
Revelation 2:1–7

In his book *Missionary Methods: St. Paul's or Ours,* Roland Allen says that the secret of Paul's missionary strategy, on the human side, was his concern for "strategic centers." Every city in which Paul did major work was a center of Roman administration, Greek civilization, Jewish influence, and world commerce. From these strategic centers the Christian witness radiated outward until it permeated the nations. This is advice we could well follow today.

If we were to pick out the world's most strategic cities of today, what ones would we list? Just for fun, let me list a few by continents without saying why:

Europe: London, Paris, Rome, Bohn, Berlin.

Asia: Moscow, Tokyo, Peiping, New Delhi.

The Middle East: Cairo, Beirut, Tel Aviv.

Africa: Johannesburg, Salisbury.

South America: Rio de Janeiro, Buenos Aires, Sao Paulo.

North America: Washington, D. C., New York, Los Angeles, New Orleans.

We have looked at three major cities and churches of the first century: Jerusalem, Philippi, and Thessalonica. We would do well to consider Corinth, Rome, and others. But we are going to skip over to the seven churches mentioned in Revelation. Each was a strategic city and church of the first century, although none is of any importance today. Could it be that our own great cities and church will be nothing but remembered historic ruins tomorrow? If so, in what way will we be remembered?

The letters to the seven churches make up the most familiar portion of the book of Revelation. Each letter is intended for each church, that is, one is for all and all are for one. The individuality of each church is recognized and respected. Yet, each church belongs to the wider circle of the Christian fellowship. They are individual churches, but they are interrelated.

You see, the idea of the autonomy of the local church is basically good. This is the way it should be. But never has any one church lived in isolation, in separation from other churches. Churches need each other.

We Baptists stress the congregational nature of the church more than any other group, with two exceptions: the Disciples of Christ and the Congregationalists (now known as the United Church of Christ). Nevertheless, we have learned that we cannot go it alone. We have associations, state conventions, regional-national conventions, and a world alliance. While we have banded with each other, we have been slow, too slow, in finding fellowship and cooperative unity with other Christians. We Southern Baptists, for example, are the only Baptist group in the world that has no part of either the National or World Council of Churches. Many of us feel that not only do we have a strong witness to offer these councils, but that we could gain by participation. We do not need union, but we could use unity.

John begins with Ephesus, not only for geographical and political reasons but also because this was the most important church in the province. Forty years earlier Paul had spent three years of his ministry at Ephesus. In the closing decade of the first century, it seems to have been the literary center of Asiatic

Christianity, from which came not only Revelation, but also the Gospel and Epistles of John, and maybe even the pastoral epistles. Twenty years later Ignatius wrote his first and longest letter to Ephesus.

Ephesus was one of the most important and interesting cities of the Roman Empire. It was a sort of hub where the crossroads of world commerce came together, both by sea and land. Therefore, it was a center of business and trade. Founded about a thousand years before Christ by colonists from Athens, successive people left their mark upon the city. Under liberal Roman rule, which began about 190 B.C., Ephesus became a racial melting pot, a cosmopolitan center, and a religious battlefield.

From the days of Croesus in 560 B.C., the worship of a fertility goddess dominated the city. In Paul's day this goddess was called Diana, and the Temple of Diana was considered one of the seven wonders of the ancient world.

Ephesus was a city of trade guilds, culture societies, and varied organizations. There were factions, rivalries, jealousies, and rancor. Each group was seeking its own ends, for its own furtherance, regardless of the effect on anyone else. Thus, they were easy prey for anyone who would stir up discontent by pitting one group against another.

Many nations of today's world face this kind of group rivalry. Our own country has been relatively free of it. However, there is developing a strong tendency in the United States to pit one group against another as each seeks its own selfish ends.

There is the labor versus management conflict: Specific veteran's organizations are being based on religion. In politics there are efforts to balance a ticket by religious and ethnic selections, or with racial balances. All of what is classified as "Black Power" is serving to further divide and alienate. We need to learn that such things lead to dissension and division.

In the cosmopolitan atmosphere of fabulously wealthy Ephesus, with all of the crosscurrents of interests and conflicts of loyalty, the people—some of them at least—recognized that Paul's religious-ethical message about a way of life made sense. The people listened to him in their synagogues, schools, homes, and the marketplace. His message won some converts. In spite of opposition, Paul recognized that Ephesus offered an open door for the gospel to go out into all of Asia Minor.

Ephesus was perhaps the strongest center of Christianity in the later part of the first century. Founded by Paul in approximately A.D. 52, this church was regarded as the leading church of the province. It was at Ephesus that Paul wrote his first epistle to the Corinthians, which contained that classic statement about love. Priscilla and Aquila were associated with this church, as was Erastus, John the Apostle of Love, and John the Presbyter. Therefore, from the beginning, the church at Ephesus was well grounded in the Christian doctrine of love. Thus her departure is all the more surprising. Yet, with the passing of the years, the ardor of Christian love had been lost. The church at Ephesus offers us both an example and a warning about what happens when an outside force and internal bickering cause the church to lose sight of its first objective and reduce the warmth of Christian activity based on love.

Another reason this church is addressed first by John is not necessarily because of its own importance but because the warning itself is so vital. At first the Ephesians showed up well. They resisted all threats to the purity of their faith from outside persons who came claiming to be apostles and from insiders who adopted the Nicolaitan ideas.

The charge against the Ephesians is that their intolerance of imposture, their hatred of heresy had bred an inquisitorial spirit which left no room for honest difference in love. As defenders of the faith, they had lost the one quality without which all the other qualities were worthless. The zeal for Christian truth had obliterated the one truth that matters—*that God is love.* John shares their hatred of heresy, but he recognizes the appalling danger of a religion prompted more by hatred than by love. The only legitimate hatred is a revulsion against all that thwarts the operation of love, and how easily hatred can be turned into something less innocent. For all its apparent strength and vigor, this church is in danger of losing its *lamp,* and thus cease being a real church.

The warning given to Ephesus is the same that is given to Laodicea, the last of the seven churches to whom John wrote. The warning could be stated this way: Churches must be on guard, lest they lose the essential qualities of their inner faith and thus affect their outward practice.

Now, let us look at the reputation of the church at Ephesus under five headings:

1. Loyal in Practice
2. Loyal in Doctrine
3. Lacking in Motive
4. The Remedy
5. The Result

First, then, *loyal in practice:* "I know your doings, your hard work, your patient endurance."

This was an active, aggressive congregation. They were engaged in active service. The word "toil," which is also translated as "hard work," implies an effort produced at the cost of pain. In other words, they actually made personal sacrifices in doing their work.

I do not mean to be facetious at this point, but there is a tongue-in-cheek mood in what I say. If we were to compare the church at Ephesus with a typical Southern Baptist church, they would be loyally cooperative in every endeavor. They would adopt all the slogans:

"Debt Free in '53"

"A Million More in '54"

"Lots to Do in '62"

"Every Baptist a Tither"

They would know all about the Cooperative Program, the Hundred Thousand Club, Lottie Moon, and they would be simultaneous to the core.

They would study the right book in the right month.

The denominational calendar would be followed to the date.

The planning books would be followed to the letter.

They would meet all the standards.

They would know it took ten visits to enlist a new person.

They would know that the church grew at the rate of one worker for each ten people.

They would know that the Sunday School multiplied by division. There would be no sitting on their hands, no sitting around waiting for people to come, no such statements as: "They know where the church is, if they want to come." They worked; *and worked hard!* Would that our church would follow some of these procedures and that our people worked in like manner. If we could just graft on that kind of work to our freewheeling concept and keep our same spirit.

The late Professor Hal Luccock of Yale had a mythical church which he called "the Church of St. Vitus." This would describe Ephesus: It is a church in motion, and that is something for which to get on your knees, and thank heaven. . . . The catch is that so much effort is given to getting up momentum that there is none left to consider a destination . . . with here a quota, there a quota, everywhere a quota. The hum of the machinery rarely dies down so that old words may be heard:

'Be still, and know that I am God.' There are Sundays when the goal for the week—a 25 per cent increase . . . does not quite meet the needs of hungry hearts or of lives that have come to the end of the map." [1]

In the second place, Ephesus was *loyal in doctrine:* "I know that you cannot bear wicked men, and you have tested those who style themselves apostles [no apostles they!] and have detected them to be liars."

This was indeed a word of praise, for it was earned by their constancy in the face of hostility from their pagan fellow Christians. Some Christian groups of that day were on easy terms with their pagan neighbors, adopting many of their practices and adapting themselves to the local environment. Corinth is such an example. But not Ephesus! They kept themselves free from all taint of evil practice and false teachings.

Several years ago Dr. Herschel Hobbs, pastor in Oklahoma City and past president of the Southern Baptist Convention, wrote an article entitled "Orthodoxy vs. Orthopraxy" in which his theme was for us to practice what we preach. He said that no system of belief is any better than the people who practice it. Said Dr. Hobbs: Let one of our churches sprinkle a baby . . . and it is immediately declared out of order and its New Testament orthodoxy is questioned . . . But a good, orthodox, New Testament church can report no baptisms year after year and remain a good, orthodox New Testament church. This thing ought not to be so. Orthodoxy must be equaled by orthopraxy.

The people of Ephesus could sharply distinguish and discriminate between loyalty and disloyalty, good and evil, true prophets and false. But the first rapture of their devotion to Christ had waned. They were doctrinally loyal, but they had lost the motivation of love and the glow of warm human compassion. They were good seed in shallow ground.

This is always a dangerous situation, when the creative spirit dies; yet, it is an experience we face everywhere.

A young athlete works hard to make the team, makes it, then lets up. I know what this is in my own family. In junior high school my son was a new boy at McMain. There were twenty-two boys trying out for two places on the basketball squad. He made it. Then he set his sights on making the starting team. He made that for the first game, loafed, and was benched for the second game. He did the same thing at the University of Tennessee, lettering as a freshman, then, a sorry sophomore year.

A businessman struggles to achieve success; he does succeed and goes up the ladder fast, then he coasts.

If honest confession is good for the soul, let me confess. Some years ago I set myself to the task of writing. It was thrilling. I enjoyed it, worked hard, had many things published, and achieved the goal I had set for myself. Then inertia set in. I still wanted to write, to see my name in print. But motivation was lacking. It came back. The weak flesh got motivated again.

This same thing happens to a church. Look at us. For years we dreamed of a much needed building. Then we built. What next? Ease in Zion? It better not be! We still have a debt of $300,000 to pay. And that means hard work, harder now than when we built in 1962.

Some ten years after my graduation from Yale Divinity School a former professor, Dr. Richard Niebuhr, spoke to a group of alumni. He said: "Never let the prophet's flame of fire become merely a smoldering ember." What a warning for a person and to a church.

So, we come to the problem of Ephesus, *lacking in motive*. "But I have this against you: You have given up loving one another as you did at first."

The church had departed from the fervor of love which had

characterized their first experience as Christians. Their fire had become smoking embers. They were carrying on the activities of an aggressive church, but they had gone away from the right motive of worship and service. Work without worship is worthless. Likewise, worship without work is not true worship. Worship and service are never either/or, but always both/and, just as faith and works are two sides of the same coin. They go together.

It is possible for all the machinery of a church to be in full, well-greased working order, while at the same time the spirit of love is absent so that the grit of irritation gets in and causes the machinery to grind to a halt which then leads to decline.

The reason for the criticism of lack of motive is that a program is considered more important than people. A civic club can work hard for credit on its annual achievement report and lose sight of the true motive of civic betterment, the reason for the club's existence. A person may even contribute to the church for an income tax deduction instead of being motivated by the Christian teaching of stewardship.

This whole matter of motivation requires a close look. There is no point in having a meeting just to have a meeting. There is no point in having an organization merely to be able to display a placard. It is awfully easy, especially among us Baptists, to get the impression that we plug away at meetings, programs, and organizations because it is expected of us. It is equally easy for us to forget that our primary ministry and concern is people. Programs and organizations are necessary; we cannot do without them, but they need constant evaluation in light of what is our motivation.

My understanding of the Bible is that God has always been more concerned with our motives than our motions, more with our attitudes than our actions, and more with our devotion than our deeds. Someone used the picturesque description of the sap leaving the tree which causes the foliage to wither so that death descends from leaf to branch to root. To all outward appearances the tree is alive. But the inner source of life and power are gone. Death and decay come slowly without the inner supply of life; but they come surely. And this was happening to Ephesus.

Come, now, and consider *the remedy:* ". . . remember the heighth from which you have fallen; repent and act as you did at first." Here, then, is a threefold remedy.

First, remember past experiences. We should never forget the past, just so we do not live in the past. The early joy, and there is a joy that comes with the initial Christian experience, needs to be recalled time and again. The zest of the Christian life, and that's a good word—*zest,* may it never depart from us.

Maybe we have forgotten, if we ever knew, the divine force of love. Perhaps we are afraid of what might happen, or we are unprepared to demonstrate real Christian love. The world has always been amazed and astounded at any demonstration of Christian love. One of the New Testament sentences says: "See how these Christians love one another." Louie Newton of Atlanta once said: "The Christian must out think, out live, and out love the rest of the world." I like that.

The second portion of the remedy is repent, change, start a new course, a new direction. Every church and every Christian needs a periodic examination. We visit the doctor and the dentist for regular checkups, or we should. We give our cars five-thousand mile inspections. We look over our insurance programs. Why not do the same to our spiritual life and to our church life?

The third portion of the prescription is "act as you did at first." That is, return to the early condition of joy by changing and eliminating those conditions that are smothering life. We can do this by: praying more, getting out into the so-called highways and hedges where the people are with their hungry hearts and needs, and sharing our experience with someone else. This is the surest way I know to cure the spiritual disease of apathy, or atrophy, or dissipation, or whatever we may have.

Finally, *the result:* "The conqueror I will allow to eat from the tree of life."

One of the easiest places in the Christian faith for us to get our motives mixed up is at this point. Certainly, I believe that the Christian will have eternal life with God. But it is awfully easy for us to have as our motive for being a Christian one of "fire insurance protection" or "whole life coverage." Yes, the security of heaven for the believer is assured by God. But there is far more:

"If you love me, keep my commandments."

"A new commandment I give to you, that you love one another."

"We know that we have passed from death to life, because we love the brethren.

This kind of love is to be seen in our attitude toward people, our courage to transform society, and in our own spiritual life, that is, what we do outside of church.

NOTES

1. Simeon Stylites, "The Twelve Worst Churches." Copyright 1951 Christian Century Foundation. Reprinted by permission from the March 7, 1951 issue of *The Christian Century*.

CHAPTER SIX:

Smyrna, Political Opportunism
Revelation 2:8–12

Forty miles from Ephesus on the Aegean Sea stood, and still stands, the city of Smyrna, with a seaport great enough to rival Ephesus, which it ultimately surpassed. Founded in the twelfth century before Christ by the Greeks, Smyrna had grown rich in trade between Asia and the West. Its public buildings rivaled those of Ephesus and Pergamum. It was a prosperous and progressive city.

The land around the area was fertile. Grape vineyards were in abundance. Significantly, Bacchus, the god of wine and revelry, was the god most honored. The beauty of the city earned it such names as "Lovely One," "The Crown of Ionia," and "The Ornament of Asia."

Smyrna was a hardy city in that on more than one occasion it was destroyed by earthquake or fire and each time it had rebuilt in larger proportions and more beauty. The ancient Greek city was destroyed about six hundred years before Christ and was never rebuilt. Instead, a new city on the coast was planned by Alexander the Great and built by his successors. The description by John of Christ as the first and the last, who was dead and came to life, is well suited to a city which had also been dead and came back to life and which now claimed to be "first." Smyrna was the last city in Asia Minor to yield to the Moslem conquest, being conquered by Tamerlane in A.D. 1402. Today it is known by the name of Izmir and is an important seaport of Turkey.

Nothing is known of the origin of the church. Twenty years after the writing of Revelation, Ignatius stayed there and wrote four of his letters. A little later, from Troas, Ignatius wrote two letters, one to the church and one to Bishop Polycarp.

There was a large Jewish population in Smyrna. These Jews were exceedingly friendly toward Rome. Interested in material wealth, they were eager to stay on good terms with the governmental authorities. Strange as it may seem, the Jews had helped build a statue to the Emperor Tiberias. These same Jews were especially hostile to the Christians, although many, if not most, of the Christians there were Jews.

The first persecution of the Christians at Smyrna came from the Jews. This hostility was regrettable but not surprising. Even the Christians retaliated against the Jews. (This was not in accord with Jesus' teaching about turning the other cheek, but perhaps they had turned their cheeks several times.) One writer, in commenting on this Christian retaliation, deplores this as being the first display of anti-Semitism. But I cannot see this accusation and will not accept this as anti-Semitism. After all, most of the people were Semitic, and many of them were Jews. This is too much of a reading of twentieth-century ideas into a first-century situation. In our own day one can hardly quote historical data for fear of being branded as anti-Semitic, or anti-something. There are efforts, even among some Christians, to cease trying to get a Jew to become a Christian. No Christian should ever apologize for trying to convert a Jew, a Moslem, or anyone else to faith in Christ. Nor, for that matter, should they apologize for their own efforts to convert others, not if we or they actually believe what we profess.

The church at Smyrna seems to have come the nearest of all to being the ideal church. It is one of two for which John has unqualified praise. Only Smyrna and Philadelphia were unrebuked. These Christians were praised more than any other group. They were subjected to active hostility, instigated in the main by the Jews. Their poverty might have been due in part to mob violence and looting and partly due to the difficulty of making a living in an antagonistic environment. Even today Christians in Moslem cities have that same problem as do many Protestants in some sections of South America.

Christians in other cities had been familiar with Jewish resentment, occasioned by the conversion of Jews to Christianity. But at Smyrna and Philadelphia this resentment was apparently more virulent than usual. John tries to prepare his friends for their persecution in three ways: they are to recognize the attack as the work of Satan; any offer to compromise is an onslaught on their integrity; and they are to remain loyal, even if they die.

In some respects, this congregation holds more interest for us than any other. Not only is it interesting because of its high moral and spiritual standing but also on account of the historical details that are preserved in writings outside the New Testament. For example, Polycarp, one of the earliest Christian martyrs, lived in Smyrna. Polycarp was put to death about the year A.D. 156. He said that he had served Christ for eighty-six years; so he must have become a follower of Christ about the year A.D. 70.

For our purposes, let us say that the book of Revelation was written about A.D. 96. Polycarp would have been a Christian some twenty-six years at the time of the writing. He claimed to have been a disciple of the apostle John; so Polycarp must have been Bishop of Smyrna when Revelation was written. Furthermore, Ignatius, who was pastor at Antioch, writing in the year

A.D. 108, said that he found Polycarp was the overseer of the church at Smyrna.

Now, let's take a look at the reputation of the church at Smyrna and see what we can find to bring some contact between the first and twentieth centuries.

For one thing, it was a *slandered* church: "I know your tribulation and your poverty . . . and the slander of those who say they are Jews and are not, but are of the synagogue of Satan."

Tribulation and poverty were the chief trials of the Christians at Smyrna; but these were the common lot of most Christians of the time. Perhaps the wealth of the Jews was such a contrast to the poverty of the Christians that there was an obvious distinction. No doubt the Christians were taunted with such statements as: "See, if you hadn't become a Christian, you'd be working, making a good income, and not having all these problems."

If it is true that we should beware when all men speak well of us, then is the opposite also true? Are we to be encouraged if all men speak ill of us and slander us? Not necessarily so, but if so, then Smyrna was on the top of the shelf.

The Roman Government accused the Christians of sedition and disloyalty. The Jews joined the Romans as they accused Polycarp of hostility toward the state. Many Christian groups are being so accused today. To be a Baptist in Russia, for example, is not easy. Did you see the news story of the Russian who was accused of being a Baptist because he neither drank nor smoked? He had a hard time convincing the authorities that he was *not* a Christian.

In many of the newer nations, especially in Africa, Christians are looked upon as suspect. They are told: "Christianity is the white man's religion. You don't want anything to do with that!"

Even here in the United States our own government has made

some severe restrictions against some Christian groups, such as the Amish people and the Jehovah's Witnesses. This despite our concept of religious liberty. And have we Baptists come to their aid, or have we forgotten our own early hard times?

The morality of these Smyrna Christians was also questioned. It is strange, but all too often when there is nothing to attack about a person, some questions concerning the person's morality are raised. And there is usually someone around quoting the old cliche, "Where there's smoke, there's fire," never considering *who started the smoke*. Society scorned them as Christians. The Jews then accused them of blasphemy. The questioning of doctrinal orthodoxy is another technique often used to discredit someone with whom there is disagreement. You see, people of all sorts were tearing their reputation to shreds. Personally, I don't like such tactics anywhere by anyone.

In the second place, it was a *persecuted* church: "I know your tribulation." Jesus had said, "When you have suffered persecution for my sake, you are blessed; for the kingdom of heaven belongs to you."

Persecution is a natural outgrowth of slander. You just cannot keep hearing or saying mean things about a person or a group for very long until you get to believing what is said and heard. Then words are not enough. If the person is all that bad, get his hide and nail it to the wall! Acts of violence have to be committed.

The persecution was begun by the Jews and then taken up by the Romans. The slanderers incited the mob into action. Mobs are always dangerous. They add anonymity; they add bravery. Many a man in a mob will do evil deeds that he would abhor and never dream of doing alone. I read a clever expression of this truth: "When the big dog is down, all the little dogs will jump on the pile."

Not all persecution and slander result in physical harm and violence. Churches can be maligned in other ways that are just as devastating. Here are a few examples:

The Olin T. Binkley Memorial Baptist Church of Chapel Hill, North Carolina, was refused membership in the local association of Baptist churches but was admitted to the North Carolina Baptist Convention.

The University Baptist Church in Baton Rouge was for a time kept out of the Judson Association because it preferred its own statement of faith to that adopted by the 1964 Southern Baptist Convention. This despite Section 3 of the introduction to that 1964 Statement, which reads: "That any group of Baptists, large or small have the inherent right to draw up for themselves and publish to the world a confession of their faith whenever they may think it advisable to do so."

A Baptist association in Charlotte, North Carolina, withdrew fellowship from two churches because some in the association did not like the baptismal practices of those churches.

The Arkansas Baptist Convention has done the same thing to churches in disagreement over both baptism and Lord's Supper practices although the convention accepts money from the churches.

The 1969 meeting of the American Baptist Convention, lest you think this method is entirely limited to the South, tried to pass a rule that no delegates could be seated from any church unless they had been properly immersed. This was defeated.

The Texas Baptist Convention acted maturely in 1969 by refusing to adopt any policies regarding the practices of an individual Baptist church.

It is a sad day when any church, or group of churches, tries to belittle or dictate to another church.

Another factor about the church was its *poverty:* "I know

your poverty, (but you are rich . . .)." How many of us today would say: Because we are Christians, we are rich? Although Gladys Salassi did tell us about the man who spoke at a pre-Southern Baptist Convention session saying that because he loved Jesus he was a financial success, his wife was beautiful, and his daughter made cheerleader and the dean's list. Or how many of us would prefer our Christian faith to material wealth, if we had to choose, that is?

Most of us are interested in a both/and instead of an either /or. But what if it did have to be either/or? In some places of the world, as I've said, Christians cannot find employment, or are kept from the better jobs, and young people are denied education. You can read Finlay Graham's mission study book, *Sons of Ishmael,* and learn that.

I had a long-time acquaintance in Americus, Georgia, Dr. Clarence Jordon, who just died a few weeks ago. Clarence Jordon was as devout and humble a Christian as I have ever known. As a collegian, I heard him at Ridgecrest and have never fully escaped some of his influence. A native of Georgia, graduate of the University of Georgia, with a doctor's degree in New Testament Greek from the Southern Baptist Seminary in Louisville, Kentucky, he translated the New Testament in what is called *The Cotton Patch New Testament. The Christian Century* called his Koinonia Farm in Americus the nearest thing to a New Testament community it had ever seen. Few men suffered any more persecution and slander than Clarence Jordon. It brought him to poverty. His business was bombed and burned, his home was attacked and bombed, insurance companies cut him off, the police offered him no protection, he became literally bankrupt.

But, my soul! What a radiant faith shined in his darkness.

Perhaps Clarence Jordon did go to what some call extremes

in his expression of Christian conviction. What matter? His fellow Christians should not have added to his troubles, causing him to suffer for his convictions.

The temptation to abandon a faith that was costing everything must be strong, whether in Smyrna or in Americus, especially when by abandoning such faith status and property could be regained. But neither Smyrna nor Americus would abandon their faith. They were held by it. They would not let it go.

Briefly, a fourth thing: It was a church with a *dark future:* "Behold, the devil is about to throw some of you into prison, that you may be tested." We should at least expect the writer to hold out some hope for them. But not yet. Things were to get worse before they would get better. Henry C. Sheldon's *History of the Church* tells of the martyrdom of some of the people at Smyrna: "Some were thrown to the wild beasts. Some were burned at the stake . . . but the grace given to the martyrs was equal to their suffering."

In the face of all this, how could one call them a *rich* church? ". . . but you are rich . . . fear not. Be faithful unto death and I will give you a crown of life."

Fear is a pesky emotion. It is necessary and can be very valuable. Yet, there is something shattering and disintegrating about fear. It can tear us up as well as cause us to stand firm. As the clouds, foreboding and dark, gathered and descended upon the church at Smyrna, the Great Voice spoke: "Fear not!"

That strange man, Soren Kirkegaard, the father of the school of thought called neo-orthodoxy as well as of the modern philosophical school of existentialism, seemed to think that suffering and pain were essential to Christianity. But there is no trace of eagerness for pain in the New Testament. Sought-for-martyrdom was a later development.

In the New Testament, pain and suffering are tragic evils

which the Christian meets in a world where there are many elements of hostility. But Christ can keep the Christian from fear of these hostile forces and will enable the Christian to live a life of triumph in the midst of them. "Fear not" is one of the most characteristic phrases to be found in the New Testament.

How could they be called rich? Certainly their riches were not in the realm of material possessions. They were rich in the possession of a Savior who had not given them a spirit of fear but a spirit of the kind of love that casts out fear and brings self-control. They were rich in the possession of convictions which they felt were worth living for, and if necessary worth dying for. Anyone who possesses a purpose which makes life meaningful is rich. They were rich in the possession of a spirit of good will and love that slander and persecution cannot destroy. When they were hated, they refused to give way to hate. When they were lied about, they dealt in truth. When reviled, they did not seek vengeance. To have met the enemy on the enemies' ground would have lowered them to the level of their adversaries. And they refused to be dragged down. They were rich in possessing a quality of life over which neither slander, persecution, poverty, nor death had destructive power.

Note this word of encouragement: "Be faithful unto death, and I will give you the crown of life."

The crown promised to the faithful is that crown which belongs to eternal life; it is the symbol of that reward which is granted to all the faithful at the end of this earthly life.

Smyrna was famous for its games, some of them quite bloody. Thousands of spectators would come to see the gladiators do battle, duels to the death. The crowds cheered wildly when the winner was presented a crown symbolic of his reward as "the most valuable gladiator" of the contest.

The church was in a duel with the Roman Empire. All the

forces of hostile evil were arrayed against them. These Christians were not asked to win the battle in their own strength; they *were* asked to be faithful, even if it meant death. Then God would award the crown, eternal life.

Let us not frown and fuss with them about being preoccupied with "things to come." Let us remember their situation of trouble. Let us remember that in times of persecution and hardship hope for a better future always seems more important than it seems to those of us who face no trouble. In World War II, for example, what did we do? We stressed the "good life" that would come after the war; a good life in terms of things and gadgets. Now we have it so good that we are not concerned. You see, it is a lot harder to face good times than it is hard times.

Come now to the refrain, or theme, of this symphony of the church: "He who has an ear, let him hear what the Spirit says to the churches."

Ah, how easy it is for distance, both of time and geography, to throw a romantic halo over the past. We sing a hymn with these lines:

> Our fathers chained in prisons dark,
> Were still in heart and conscience free:
> How sweet would be their children's fate,
> If they, like them, could die for Thee!

But do we *really* mean that? Remember, *we* are the children! Evidently, we do not mean it, for this verse has been omitted from the current edition of our own *Baptist Hymnal*.

Earlier I referred to Polycarp, one of the early Christian martyrs. In the year A.D. 156, a cruel persecution broke out. The people made Polycarp go into hiding. His enemies forced a child to reveal his hiding place. Today's Communists use this same technique in causing children to be informers, even against their own parents. When apprehended, the old Christian said: "The will of God be done."

He came from hiding to meet his captors, ordered refreshments for them (typical of the Middle East hospitality), and asked for one favor, which was granted: that he might have one hour alone. All that Polycarp needed to do to save his life was to offer a sacrifice to the Emperor of Rome. But coming from his hour of prayer he said: "Eighty and six years have I served Christ, and he has never done me wrong; how, then, can I curse him, my King and Saviour?"

So, Polycarp was burned at the stake in Smyrna. Such an attitude has been with Christians for these twenty centuries. Who can ever forget Martin Niemoller of Germany? or Bishop Bergraav of Norway? The Nazis changed Bergraav's guard every three days so as to keep them from falling under his influence. Dr. William Wallace, one of our medical missionaries, was martyred in Communist China. More than seventy Protestant missionaries have lost their lives in Colombia in the past two decades.

What was it Paul said? "I bear in my body the marks of the Lord Jesus" (Gal. 6:17). We read in Polycarp's martyrdom prayer: "O Lord, Almighty God, the Father of Thy beloved Son, Jesus Christ, through whom we have received a knowledge of Thee, God of the angels and the whole creation, of the whole race of man, and of the saints who live before Thy presence; I thank Thee that Thou hast thought me worthy, this day and this hour, to share the cup of Thy Christ among the numbers of Thy witnesses."

CHAPTER SEVEN

Pergamum, Social Conformism

Revelation 2:12–17

The modern city of Bergama in western Turkey can trace its origin to the ancient city called Pergamum. Pergamum, as a city, attained the peak of its culture some two hundred years before Christ, coming to prominence after the death of Alexander the Great, when it became the capital of a new, independent state. It did not owe its importance to commerce, as did Ephesus and Smyrna. Rather, it was a center of culture and religion. These two things are often found in combination, both in the past and today.

Our own Crescent City could qualify on three scores, for we have had commerce, culture, and religion. We are reminded by the Cultural Attractions Fund that New Orleans had culture when the rest of the United States had agriculture. We were the first city in the New World to have our own opera house and symphony orchestra. Even now we are one of the few cities in the nation to have both an opera and a symphony. Let's keep it that way, and develop all of our cultural attractions.

Religiously, the Roman Catholic Church has made New Orleans one of its major areas of North America. The oldest established cathedral in the United States is St. Louis, established here in 1794. The Greek Orthodox Cathedral of the Holy Trinity is the oldest church of that faith on the North American continent. Protestants have not been here so long. The first Protestant service was in November, 1805. But our growth, especially in the past two decades, has been remarkable.

In commerce, we are ideally situated. The mighty Mississippi connects us with the heartland of America. Our port is the second largest in the nation. We are the natural outlet to South America. But, once known as the "Queen City of the South," we no longer have that reputation. Atlanta, Houston, and Dallas are surpassing us. And I, for one, do not like it. We should never abdicate our prized position.

But, let's get back to Pergamum. Religiously, Pergamum had three major temples: one to Zeus, the chief god of all the gods in the pantheon; one to Aphrodite, the goddess of love, beauty, war, and the underworld (And that's quite a combination for one goddess!); And one to Aescalapious, the serpent-god who presided over the art of healing—medicine.

Here again New Orleans is much like Pergamum. We have Rex as our chief god, and Rex gets so large a proportion of the city's attention that there's little time, energy, or money left for other developments. Much of our reputation, especially as a tourist attraction, centers around the worship of Aphrodite on Bourbon Street and the parasitic tenacles of organized crime. We are one of the nation's major medical centers, although the reputations of our two medical schools are dangerously slipping. As the serpent was one of Pergamum's symbols, so Caduceus, the figure of a serpent twined around a staff, is the modern symbol of the medical profession.

You see, patron saints for a city are no new thing. They are a carry over from paganism. Today's ruins of Pergamum reveal a hillside theater near the shrine of Aescalapious which would seat thirty-five hundred people. So, Loudres, St. Anne de Beaupre, and Oral Roberts are nothing new.

The thirteenth verse of the second chapter of Revelation mentions "Satan's throne," or "the place where Satan dwells." This could have been a reference to the great altar to Zeus, built on the city's acropolis. It stood on a base one hundred feet square, and rose fifty feet high. This altar was excavated in the nineteenth century and taken to the Berlin museum.

Had Paul visited Pergamum, he could have used the same sermon he used on Mars Hill in Athens: "Men of Pergamum, I perceive that you are very religious."

Culturally, one of the largest libraries of the ancient world was located at Pergamum. It contained over two hundred thousand volumes. This library rivaled the one of Ptolemy in Alexandria, Egypt. Ptolemy feared that his prized library would be overshadowed, so he forbade the export of papyrus to Pergamum. (Economic sanctions and blockades are no new thing, either!) To offset this ban, Pergamum turned its scientists loose on research, and they came up with a substance known as parchment made from the skin of sheep and goats. And Pergamum became the center of bookmaking—the publishing of books, that is, not the race track bookmaking for which our city is known. (They might have made "book" on the chariot races, though.) You see, we are not so modern when we think that we can withhold our secrets about atomic energy, or anything else for that matter. Other scientists are not so dumb. They make their own discoveries. Yet, we go on our ostrich-like way.

It would be interesting to know who founded the Christian community in this city, when, and under what circumstances. Unfortunately, we do not know. We would like to have some sidelights about the church, such as about Polycarp and the church at Smyrna. But we know nothing. All we know is found in six brief verses in Revelation, plus what we can learn about the historical setting of the city.

Just what could we say about our own church in so little space and so few words that two thousand years from now people could know something about us or even be interested in us?

As we consider the reputation of the church at Pergamum, let's look at the good things first.

"I know where you dwell, where Satan's throne is." John believed that Rome was the latest and greatest agent of Satan, not only because of Rome's totalitarian demands for that absolute allegiance which belongs to God alone but also because he saw in Rome the epitome of all paganism and worldliness. No better expression of this could be found than in the many religious monuments of Pergamum.

The Roman governor of Asia was a pro consul with an almost unlimited command of which the symbol was a sword. This explains the imagery of the opening sentence: "The words of him who has a sharp two-edged sword." The Christians are reminded that though they live under the authority of one who holds the sword of imperial law, they are also citizens of the greater empire of him who needs no other weapon than the "sword of his words," that is, the spoken word of God.

Those Christians were keeping the faith in the midst of the most difficult situation imaginable—right in the midst of Satan's headquarters: the seat of Emperor worship, the place of many gods. But, there are always "saints in Caesar's household." There are Christians in Peiking, Moscow, Havana, Hanoi, *and* in New Orleans!

"You hold fast my name." That is, you have been true to me personally. This was a loyal, steadfast, dependable church. Sharing in the faith of Christ, they also shared the courage of Christ in holding to some convictions even if others disagreed.

We talk a lot about having the courage to live by our convictions, but see what we do to those whose convictions are contrary to ours. We speak about the "right of dissent," but see how we treat the dissenters. Even we Baptists, who preach this doctrine with vigor and extol the virtues of our fathers who practiced it, are quick to deny its validity to our fellowmen. See how associations and state conventions deal with churches whose opinions about baptism and the Lord's Supper are different. Listen as a past president of the Southern Baptist Convention told those who interpret Baptist doctrines differently from him to "get out" and find another church home.

"You did not deny my faith" suggests that some had actually been asked to do just that. The pressure to deny their faith came not only from Rome but also from public pressure. Remember, Peter denied Jesus without being charged in any court or even asked by any individual to do so. There must have been many occasions in Pergamum when it was "politic" not to be openly recognized as a Christian.

But they clung to their faith despite opposition in the midst of a sophisticated intellectualism and even in the center of the pagan worship of many gods. Even when one of their members, Antipas, was killed, they remained firm.

Let's back up, take a look, and ask some questions about the church itself. Why was there a church at Pergamum? When did it become known as Satan's headquarters and why? Was this before or after the establishment of the church? How did Pergamum get its reputation?

It may have been that Pergamum had been Satan's greatest stronghold for many years. If so, then the church had been established, not because of the promise of building a great church but because the situation was so hopeless and the need was so great.

All churches ought to be established because of need. But

how willing are we to establish a church where the situation seems hopeless? Most of the time we want everything to be so correct and right that we cannot fail.

Several years ago, in his president's address to the Southern Baptist Convention, Dr. C. C. Warren remarked that we ought to double our number of churches and preaching places. There was a great deal of excitement about that; so The Thirty Thousand Movement was born, that is, establish thirty thousand new churches and preaching places in the Southern Baptist Convention.

But where? In the Greater New Orleans area we now have sixty-eight churches. That's about one for each ten thousand people—white churches and white people. Some of those churches are poorly located. About half of them are struggling to maintain existence. Do we need any more? Yes, I believe there are sections where we need a Baptist church. But there are sub-divisions where we cannot buy property, even if we had the money, and it is terribly expensive; not like Atlanta, Dallas, or Houston where a new church can begin with acres of property and hundreds of prospects.

I remember hearing Johannes Arndt of Hamburg, Germany speak at the Baptist World Alliance in London in 1955 on the text: "I will build my church." Dr. Arndt pointed out that Jesus was not speaking of building his church in some quiet, peaceful valley; it was to be built at the very gates of hell, and hell itself couldn't keep the church from being built. Arndt continued by saying that when the gates of hell are open is the *normal* time to build the church. Our concept of "normal times" is just the opposite. We want everything to be just right. But every act of Satan has but one purpose: *to destroy the work of God!* And the church must never make peace with Satan.

If the church at Pergamum was established, as Johannes

Arndt suggested, then those Christians who founded the church and were carrying on the work were doing so not because the task was easy *but because it was hard!* They had heard the call of God for those who were willing to face desperate odds, assured only that "the gates of hell will not prevail," and they answered: "Here we are; send us!"

For the benefit of the newer members of St. Charles Avenue Baptist Church, with all of our reputation of affluence, intellectualism, and "Avenue Aristocracy," let us be reminded that on April 16, 1884, we began as a mission on the corner of Maple and Cherokee in some unused servant's quarters provided by a Mrs. G. W. Haygood. It was fifteen years later that twenty-nine charter members constituted the church.

Some years before there was a church at Pergamum, a young preacher named Titus faced a similarly hard situation. In fact, he faced so many difficulties that he saw nothing else to do except "get himself called to another church as soon as possible." He wrote a letter to his friend Paul, telling him just how impossible the situation was and asked Paul to help him move.

But Paul did not encourage him to move. He agreed that Titus was in a tough spot. In fact, Paul pointed out some troubles that Titus had not recognized. Then he said: "These difficulties are no reason for you to quit, but for standing your ground. It was for this cause that I left you at Crete that you might set right the things that are wrong. If things were as they ought to be, God would not need you and me. But we are needed!"

We cannot escape some difficulties. Why should we even expect to? If we run away from one set of problems, we merely meet another set. We exchange a set of known problems for some unknown ones. Yet, most of us seem to do our best when there is a challenge, for challenges call for our best.

Today the future does not look bright for the Christian faith. Already outnumbered better than two to one, the physical birth rate annually exceeds the "new birth" rate of converts to Christianity. Moslems make more converts in Africa than do we Christians. The road ahead is rocky and steep. But, I will not concede defeat, nor will I stand idly by and let the critics of Christian faith go unchallenged. I believe in the church, for the light of God has shown in the darkness, and the darkness cannot put it out! The gates of hell will not prevail, not if the church will advance *as the church!*

One interesting surmise is that Satan set up headquarters in Pergamum because of this strong group of Christians. An interesting idea, but most unlikely. What joy it would be to think that a group of Christians was so active in making headway against the forces of evil in a city that Satan would become alarmed.

A really active church, active in being the church, always meets opposition. It should! It is a hopeful sign when the forces of evil say all manner of things against the church. That shows evil is afraid. Every victorious era of the church has been one coming out of opposition. A church which nobody fights is apt to be so trifling and useless as to be ignored.

If we Christians are meeting no opposition, if we are being ignored, then we had better check up on ourselves. Today's writing critics are not attacking the church as they once did. Usually, if they mention it at all, they merely shrug it off as being of no consequence. Modern writers are presenting all the problems of life, with little offered as solution; nor do they indicate that the church, or anyone else, has any solutions. I am afraid that, by and large, the church of today is being ignored, bypassed. Who pays any attention to what the church has to say? Who even asks its opinion?

The church at Pergamum was being opposed. And John was commending it for being faithful in a difficult situation.

Even so, the church at Pergamum was not faultless. The problem can be expressed in an earlier phrase: a tendency to make peace with Satan, that is, a social conformism. There were those in the congregation who were compromising with what is called "the heresy of the Nicolaitans." Some of the members were not too strict in their dealings with the Nicolaitans and that heresy was creeping in. They were following a lenient tolerance that was leading to moral shortcomings. As a result, the church was beginning to take on the coloring of the community; they were conforming rather than transforming.

Maybe the Nicolaitans wanted to avoid a head-on clash with Rome and believed it was possible to maintain a peaceful coexistence and not be disloyal Christians. No one could avoid all contact with paganism. But the man who believed in the one true God need not be upset by this. He could recognize that all the Romans wanted was a gesture of political loyalty.

We do not know much about the Nicolaitans. We do know that they had a tendency to take on a few of the pagan practices along with their Christianity. For example: the eating of meat which had been sacrificed to idols and sexual immorality. They reasoned that they were free from restrictions, so they would let sin abound that grace might the more abound. Since, as Christians, they were washed in the blood of the lamb, they could not be hurt spiritually by sin. That which was sin for others would not be sin for them. Was this an early form of "situation ethics"?

The practices of the Nicolaitans are compared to those of Balaam in the Old Testament. Balaam, you remember, was that character who sold out his own people, the Israelites, for a sum of money, even though it was against his better moral and religious judgment. He seemed to think that God would stay by whether the people did right or wrong. His was the sin of presumption.

There are two forms of heresy within a church, and each can be equally dangerous. First is a strict legalism with a long series of do's and don't's which make Christianity a matter of trivia and restriction rather than a vital faith. Another form of this heresy is a list of propositions to which one gives verbal assent without necessarily having the experience of a vital faith. The second form is a lenient tolerance which leads to moral short-comings. We have both kinds here in New Orleans. While I abhor the trivialities, I also deplore the lax lenience.

Not all of the Pergamum Christians were Nicolaitans, but all are warned to repent of the indifference which allowed that heresy to go unchecked. The fault of Pergamum is the opposite of Ephesus. And how narrow is that safe path between the sin of intolerance and the sin of tolerance. The peril Pergamum faced was within the church itself, which is always more danger-ous than any outside force.

Because of this tendency toward laxity, the church is called to repent of its tolerant conformism. Although they would not bow to Caesar, they were in danger of becoming too much like the society around them. So long as the enemy could be clearly identified outside the church there was little to fear. They resisted those outside attacks, even at the risk of death. But the inside peril was more subtle, more insidious, more dangerous and deadly.

To those who remain faithful, who genuinely repent, this promise is given: "To him who conquers I will give some hidden manna, and I will give him a white stone, with a new name written on it which no one knows except him who receives it."

The hidden manna is Christ. Christ not only gives new life; he is the Bread which sustains that life. The white stone has four different ancient meanings, all of which have a symbolic application to the Christian experience:

1. The white stone was given to a person who had been brought to trial and acquitted. The person would then carry that stone as a sign that he was free of the charges made against him.

2. It was given to freed slaves as an identification of citizenship.

3. It was given to the winner of a race to show that he had overcome the opposition.

4. And it was given to a soldier who returned from battle victorious over the enemy.

Do you see the picture? These Christians were given an inner manna to sustain, a white stone, and a new name to show that they were free from the guilt of sin, to identify them as citizens of Christ's kingdom, to show that they had overcome opposition, and to reveal that they had been victorious in the battle with Satan. Notice that the new name is hidden, except to those who receive it. Why? This means that there is no way to have or to sustain this new life except through personal experience, personal encounter, personal acceptance of Christ through repentance and faith.

So it is with us. There must be that personal encounter with God in Christ which points out our sin, convicts us of it, and leads us to repentance and faith in the acceptance and commitment of our lives to Jesus Christ as Savior and the identification of our lives with him and fellow believers in the church.

CHAPTER EIGHT

Thyatira, Watch that False Prophetess!
Revelation 2:18–29

Thyatira was a small city on the key highway located between Pergamum and Sardis, but just a little off the main trade route. Perhaps we could compare it to Lafayette or Lake Charles between New Orleans and Houston. The city had been founded by Alexander the Great in the third century before Christ. Today a little town in Turkey named Akhisar stands on the ancient site.

While Thyatira was not a major commercial center, there was much trade activity. There were various trade guilds (unions): bakers, potters, tanners, carvers, weavers, and dyers. The making of purple dye was a major asset. Each guild had its own god, but Apollo, the sun god, was the chief god of the city. Some commentators suggest that the reason for the phrase ". . . the Son of God, who has eyes like a flame of fire" was to show that Christ's glory was brighter than that of Apollo or even the sun itself.

The church at Thyatira was relatively small. By our current standards of measuring a church, we would probably say that it was unimportant. But no church is unimportant. Who would have ever thought that an obscure Negro Baptist church in Montgomery, Alabama, would have been the focal point of beginning one of the major movements of twentieth-century

America. But that church and its pastor, Martin Luther King, Jr., was the headquarters for the bus boycott that later grew into the Southern Christian Leadership Conference.

The Thyatira church probably began with a small group of devout Jews who came out of the large Jewish colony because they accepted Christ as the Messiah of promise. But most of the membership was composed of Gentile converts from paganism.

It is a strange phenomenon that Christianity has usually had its revival periods through acceptance of previously rejected neighbors.

In the first century Jewish Christianity was in danger of becoming an obscure Jewish sect which would probably have been absorbed in the main stream of Judaism. But when Peter went to Cornelius and when Paul and his companions saw the full impact of Christian faith and took the gospel to the Greeks and Romans, Christianity received an injection of new life that moved it into the mainstream of world history.

Later, when Rome was collapsing and the wisest Christian minds thought that the Church was failing the Empire, there were those who were considered heathen in Northern Europe who were converted to Jesus Christ and thus supplied life and future for the church.

The opening of the New World, America, provided another lease on life.

The world mission enterprise took the gospel to the uttermost parts of the world and today, particularly in Asia, the "new churches" are supplying vitality and new vigor.

Many are now asking: "What can save a decadent American Protestantism? What can free us from our captivity?" The answer is: "The Gentile!" But who is today's Gentile? Who are the dispossessed? I don't know! It may be those 'new churches' of Asia. It could be the Negro, or the poor, or even the affluent silent majority. It could even be some new movement waiting to be born.

But of this we may be sure: God will bring new life to his church from the lesser children of the earth unless we who already possess the gospel are serious in our full stewardship of it as a possession. Strange new workings of the Holy Spirit will assure the continuity of the church, whether we like it or not, whether we work with the Holy Spirit or not.

Just how the church at Thyatira was begun, we do not know. An interesting surmise is that it was started by Lydia, "a seller of purple from Thyatira," one of Paul's converts. Lydia was a brilliant, gifted woman who was converted at Philippi. Perhaps she was there on a business trip, returned home as a Christian, and started the Christian community in her home at Thyatira.

No church receives higher praise from John than the church at Thyatira. Notice his technique: When some particularly harsh criticism is to be offered it is generally prefaced with some kind words. This is a good lesson to learn. Criticism should never be purely destructive. We should always find some good in order to give hope that the bad can be overcome.

I remember my freshman English teacher at Hardin-Simmons University. There seems to be a common practice among teachers of English that indicates that they are taught to follow the same practice. I would turn in a composition to Miss Eva Rudd and she would return it with a marginal comment: "Good idea. Well written. Comma blunder. *F!*" I still wonder how anything so good, so well written could merit an *F*. There was a strange irony when, in 1958, my alma mater gave me an honorary Doctor of Literature degree, and Miss Rudd said she never thought anything like that could have happened. Fortunately, she wasn't on the committee to be allowed to ask about comma blunders in my writings. Also, a good editor helps!

No teacher ought to offer purely destructive criticism or threaten failure. No business reviews only its mistakes and losses. Our opinions of government ought not to be exclusively negative. And there is entirely too much of this going on today. And the same thing is true of the church. The theme song: "What's Wrong with the Church?" needs to be sung, of course, but the church has some good points which need mentioning, too.

Such was the case at Thyatira.

In considering the reputation of this church, let's use John's technique and look first at its good points, the things in its favor.

"I know your works . . . your love." Here is warmth and motive which was missing at Ephesus. Love was the basis of what they were doing. They were at work, not to receive credit or awards, but because they loved Christ. Their works had the passion of Christian love. This was a high word of praise. What one of us doesn't like to hear: "I know you love me. Your actions show it."

"I know your faith . . . your patience." Faithfulness is the picture of love in action, a ministry to those in need. Perhaps a better word for patience would be "steadfastness." These Christians were showing an ability to hold their own, to keep themselves from cracking under pressure. In current parlance, they were keeping their cool. Clovis Chappell once said that patience is the power to wait for a hoped-for good and the power to endure until it comes.

So often we speak of the patience of Job. But Job was not a patient man, not when he cursed the day he was born. But he was steadfast. In Jesus we have the right example of this patient steadfastness when we read: "Who for the joy that was set before him [steadfastly] endured the cross, despising the shame" (Heb. 12:2).

Those Thyatirans had a patience born of love and faith. If we love, we believe. If we believe, we can wait. If we can wait, we can endure.

"I know your later works exceed the first." This was a progressive church, not one resting on its achievements. Moral goodness, wherever it exists, is progressive, not static. Unlike all other life, the more it grows the more the craving and the larger the capacity for growth. As a church grows in love, concern, and useful service, it makes progress.

Now, with all this good, just what was wrong at Thyatira? The complaint is that the church is harboring a member who was guilty of heresy. It was the same heresy that was at Pergamum, following the Nicolaitans. The church as a whole was not guilty, but they condoned it on the part of one woman. Here again was the spirit of a lenient tolerance that did not want to hurt anyone's feelings. It is strange how much trouble one such person can cause.

A woman in the church, evidently possessing much charismatic charm, claimed to have a special revelation from God. Whenever such a claim is made, it is always time to become wary and on guard. John calls her Jezebel although that was probably not her name. Little girls just were not named Jezebel. It is more likely that her character was such that she was, as Dr. Moffatt translates, "a Jezebel of a woman."

Jezebel, you remember, was an Old Testament queen. She was not a Jewess but married King Ahab and became Queen of the Jews. She brought along with her her pagan religion, the worship of Baal and Ashtoreth. She is the worst-hated woman in the Old Testament. But the very hatred shows that she was a woman of dominate personality. Jezebel's religious influence was so strong that even Elijah felt himself to be the only worshipper of God left. Such was not the case, of course. It never is. But the situation in Israel was bad, because Jezebel was a brilliant, dashing, daring, enthusiastic woman in her religious zeal.

The woman at Thyatira is compared to the Old Testament woman. No doubt she was in an influential position and was using her prestige to spread her ideas. There is no charge of lack of Christian love against her, for the church at Thyatira had actually made progress in love and service. The charge against her closely resembles that against the Nicolaitans.

Remember, the Nicolaitan heresy was a kind of: "Go ahead, express yourself. Let yourself go. Get rid of your inhibitions. Deeds done in the body cannot hurt the soul."

Such a teaching leads some people to believe that they are above sin, that they can do no sin, no matter what their conduct may be.

In some of our situation ethics this technique may be used in such a matter as sexual seduction: "Since we love each other, and marriages are made in heaven, and in God's sight we are already married, and no one else is involved, we might as well go ahead."

The woman's teachings of "deep things" appealed to the pseudo-intellectualism of the day. And that same appeal exists among us. A system which affords at the same time both the assurance of salvation and the freedom to indulge in pleasures of the flesh makes great headway among superficial believers.

Such a teaching has a bad effect on people. It dulls the conscience, destroys sensitivity to sin, opens the door to moral ruin, and closes the eyes to watchfulness.

People were following this woman to their own ruin because

she was offering both assurance and license. Any suggestion which makes conduct irrelevant provides a perfect escape from moral responsibility.

I rather feel that we Southern Baptists have a form of the Nicolaitan heresy. When we say, "All we need to do is to get people saved. We don't need to bother about all this social gospel stuff," I believe we are in effect saying that moral, ethical conduct has nothing to do with our profession of faith. And this is not true. Our faith must produce conduct that is different from that of the one who professes no faith.

Before we are too critical of the Christians at Thyatira for their lenient tolerance and their compromises, we must remember how very difficult it was to be a Christian in a pagan society.

Plays at the theater were built around the deeds of the gods. Many times they were coarse and immoral.

The sports were bloody and inhuman. The school textbooks centered around the exploits of the gods. The sculptors made tombstones with engravings of the gods, if they did any business at all. To go to court meant to swear by false gods.

One does not appreciate the unconscious influence of a society, pagan or Christian, until he looks back on an era when Christianity was a foreign element or when he sees Christianity at work on a mission field.

The temptation to compromise was strong. Yet, compromise then, as now, meant destruction of faith. And small steps of compromise are usually more dangerous than big ones. (As a kind of aside, let me say that I fear the "small compromise" of state aid to parochial-private education here in Louisiana, or elsewhere. With all of its emotional appeals, it is a dangerous trend.) We are reminded that David Livingstone said that the creature in Africa that gave him the most trouble was not the lion, the tiger, or the crocodile *but the gnat!*

Finally, listen to what was said to the church: "I gave her time to repent, but she refuses to repent . . . I am he who searches the mind and heart, and I will give to each of you as your works deserve."

When a person refuses to repent, it means that his life is fully committed to sin. He has lost any hunger and thirst after righteousness. To have no desire, no will to repent is a tragedy we should avoid. Those who have been following Jezebel are urged to come back. Those who have been too tolerant are told to cease being indifferent. Those who have refused to give ear to her seductive voice know what they are to do in discipline.

It is a mission of the church to expel evil from its midst, from the community, to crush that which is wrong, not by force or persecution, but by the divine moral persuasion of Christian example. Christ does not will the destruction of the sinner, rather he desires that the sinner turn in repentance and be converted.

For the Christian, as for the church, it is not enough to maintain one's present position. He must advance. The church must go forward. Thyatira's later works were better than her earlier ones. For this they were praised. Now, Thyatira must continue to make progress.

So, the promise to those who do repent, who are faithful: "I will give him power. . . ." Not physical power and force, but the power to overcome evil. Broken pieces will be mended and brought together. The moral power of righteousness does bring healing to both men and nations.

"I will give him the morning star. . . ." Jesus himself comes to be the possession of him who repents. Jesus Christ, called "the Bright and Morning Star," heralds the beginning of a new life, just as the morning star says a new day is here. In a sinful world, where men live in darkness, Jesus enters as God's light, and no darkness can put out that light. And who does all this: "I am he who searches the mind."

Listen to the psalmist: "O Lord, thou hast searched me and known me . . . Search me, O God, and know my ways, and see if there be any wicked ways in me . . . Create in me a clean heart, O God, and renew a right spirit within me."

CHAPTER NINE

Saroìs, Spiritual Apathy

Revelation 3:1–6

Founded about 1200 B.C., which corresponds roughly to the date when Jericho fell to Joshua, for many years Sardis was a remarkable city in the area we know as Asia Minor. Situated on a crossroad running east and west, it was greatly enriched by commerce. It is more than coincident that good transportation facilities go hand-in-hand with the commercial progress of these ancient cities. It would seem that any city that wants industrial growth had better look to its transportation.

New Orleans is fortunate in having transportation in all its forms: water, both the river and the sea, with international port facilities; an international airport, known as "The Gateway of the Americas"; interstate and intercontinental highways; and rail facilities which go in three of the four directions of the compass. We are in an extremely favorable position, which our chamber of commerce ought to stress.

Sardis is credited with minting the first coins. Greece later took this up. (Perhaps some of you collectors may have one of those coins.) The minting process was begun under the "fantabulously" wealthy Croesus. When Cyrus captured the city about 548 B.C., it is said that he looted the city of wealth valued at $600 million.

Despite its longevity and ancient prestige, Sardis had little influence during the Roman period. A prosperous center of trade and industry, it had an *almost* impregnable acropolis to remind its citizens of departed glory. Sardis has been called by some historians a typical example of a broken-down aristocracy. The city was proud of its self-sufficiency. The attitude of the city is reflected in the people. And, unfortunately in this case, the same attitude was in the church. While Sardis was rich materially, it was bankrupt spiritually. And, sad though it is, the church reflected this spiritual poverty.

The city of Sardis was built on an acropolis with an elevation of some fifteen hundred feet. On three sides there were sheer cliffs which made it almost perfect for military defense, a sort of Golan Heights or Mossadegh. The acropolis could be reached only by a narrow strip of land on the south, and had never been captured by direct assault. But twice it had been captured by stealth, without resistance: once by Cyrus about 548 B.C., and once by Antiochus the Great in 218 B.C. On both occasions the invader had come "like a thief in the night." There seem to be two reasons for this:

First, Sardis depended upon hired mercenaries to do their fighting, unlike, say, Sparta and Athens. Its stands to reason that a soldier who is hired to fight does not have the will and dependability of one who is fighting for his homeland. If he is hired by one side, he can be bought by the other.

Second, their self-sufficiency led them to an over-confidence, which was their chief weakness. Once, while the city slept, Cyrus and his men crept up that narrow strip of land and captured the city. Some three hundred years later Antiochus did the same thing. Some folks just can't seem to learn.

A British writer recently commented on the current trend of cultural interchanges with Russia which has as its theme: "People who know each other are less likely to go to war." This is all very well. We are all desirous of anything that will make for peace. But the writer said that between 1930 and 1939 Britain and Germany had many such exchanges. While Britain got acquainted with the people, Germany made maps for future use.

You may remember your history about Quebec, or maybe you have been there. Quebec also had sheer cliffs which were considered impregnable. But General Montcalm captured Quebec. In our generation France put her military confidence in the late 1930's in her Maginot Line. But the Maginot Line did not hold much over forty-eight hours. You see, our own possession of atomic and hydrogen bombs and the ever-flying Strategic Air Command, for which I am thankful, and all of our anti-ballistic missile systems may be strong deterrents, but they are no sure-fire guarantee of security. Offensive systems have a way of counteracting defenses on both sides.

Carelessness caused Sardis to be defeated more than once. Carelessness was causing the demise of the church. Carelessness, overconfidence, is nearly always a sign of impending defeat.

At the time of the writing of Revelation, Sardis was one of the lesser cities of Asia Minor. The church had also declined to such an extent that only Laodicea was near them in low content spirituality. This letter to the church at Sardis is one of unmixed condemnation. Nothing good is said! Such a technique is the opposite of the thesis in the preceding chapter, which stated that something good should be said before criticism is offered. There were a few loyal Christians at Sardis, to be sure, but for the church as a whole no word of praise could be found. In Sardis, the majority had failed, so it is they who are addressed as being representative of the church. Here is the complaint: "I know your works; you have the name of being alive, but you are dead."

John's letter is silent about any pressures on the church from pagan religions. There were no outward signs of Satan's activities, no Jewish accusers, no imposters, no heresy, no prophetic ecstasy. This was a church which everyone spoke well of—*the perfect model of inoffensive Christianity!* This was a church unable to distinguish between the peace of well-being and the peace of death.

Someone has said that there are few things so well known and better organized than a graveyard; but there is so little life there. The church at Sardis is dead, and only the life-giving Spirit of God can bring it back to life.

What does John mean by *death?* It is wrong to picture the church at Sardis as an elderly, dwindling congregation, unable to maintain its previous activities or make new converts. The church had "the name of being alive." And this reference is not to a numerical remnant but to a residue of spiritual vitality.

Evidently, the church at Sardis was well known. Anyone in town could have told a stranger how to get to the church. A church ought to be known in a city. Says Carlyle Marney: "It is an immoral thing that a church should be so hard to find . . . Men should not have to depend upon newspaper advertising to learn its address . . . so long as men have to ask where it is it doesn't matter much where or whether it is." [1]

Sardis was even favorably known: "You have the name of being alive." People thought of it as a "live church." There is a ring of charm in this kind of reputation, for nothing is more fascinating than a live, wide-awake, active church. New people moving in to Sardis would be informed about this church. Visitors would hear about it and attend the services. But, having attended, they would feel that something is not just right. Those few loyal members likewise felt a missing element. Something was wrong. The church was not living up to its reputation.

So, what was wrong at Sardis? We have no evidence of any real enemies, no persecution, no false teachers, no heresy, no troublemakers. The church was just dead.

Why was it that neither the malice of the Jews nor the persecution of the Romans were felt at Sardis? Probably because the church had set itself to the task of avoiding hardships by pursuing a policy based on convenience rather than the zeal for truth and right. A Christianity that is robbed of its aggressiveness, enfeebled by compromised conviction, and with its distinctive message quieted by discretion neither merits nor arouses opposition.

Certainly the church was not killed by outside foes, for there was no persecution. Anyway, outside enemies have never been able to kill a church. Persecution makes friends for the persecuted *in any cause!* The blood of the martyrs has ever been the seed of the church.

Surely the death was not deliberate; nor was it murder with malice aforethought. No church member *wants* his church to die; there is no suicidal death wish. Yet this church was dead because of the spiritual apathy of its own members. That is the only way a church or any other organization ever dies.

I have a friend who is both spectacular and dramatic. One Sunday morning several years ago, just as it was time for the sermon, the local undertaker and some pallbearers wheeled in a casket and brought it to the front of the church. My friend then preached a sermon on "The Death of Mr. Prayer Meeting." At the close of the service he asked the people to come by and view the "remains." In the bottom of the casket he had placed a large mirror so that each viewer saw his own reflected image. Attendance for the next few weeks was excellent, but it slipped right back, for sensationalism is only temporary; something more theatrical has to be done.

Some time ago at our own Wednesday night service (which, by the way, is one of the strong features of our church) I used the theme: "Four Diseases That Kill a Church": "Sleeping Sickness"—asleep amid possibilities; "Cirrhosis of the Giver" —improper stewardship; "Hardening of the Heartaries"—lack of concern; "Spiritual Myopia"—seeing only the immediate. Without repeating that message, here are a few of the symptoms: People cease to pray and read the Bible, letting up on their own devotional life and spiritual nourishment.

They stop attending services regularly. They fail to give witness or testimony to others about Christ and the church. They begin saying: "Let someone else do it." As the city of Sardis hired mercenaries, the church hires staff workers to do its task. "After all, what are we paying them for?"

High Roman taxes caused them to cut their financial contributions to the church. They began giving to causes outside the church; good causes, some of them church-related. They did not give to Paul's relief offering for Jerusalem. And their mission giving was reduced.

A few wealthy people endowed the church so that there was a regular income from investments. They became proud of their past glory, their past reputation of having the "best" people, the leading citizens, the most talent of any church in town. So they neglected and paid no attention to the other folk of the community. In the past quarter of a century the growth of the Pentecostal sects in America, particularly in the South, has been phenomenal. These are the people we Baptists and Methodists used to reach and still should!

A Methodist friend of mine, Jason Shirah of Georgia, was to preach his senior sermon in the Yale Divinity School chapel. In the sermon he said: "People ask me why I want to go back South instead of staying here in New England. Well, I'll tell you: I'd rather go back South and try to restrain the fanatics than to stay up here and try to raise the dead!" That may have been a true classification twenty-five years ago, but not so true now.

Of course, all of this is the speculation of reading between the lines with imagination. We have no other evidence, other than that these things have caused present-day churches to become seriously ill. Earlier, the church at Sardis was well thought of; so they began to think well of themselves. They took on the mood of the city. They conformed rather than transforming. The Carnation cows may have to live contented lives in order to produce their best, but no contented Christian ever produces well. It is a divine discontent that causes Christian progress. Overconfidence is a familiar road to defeat. Many athletic contests have been lost because a team is overconfident. I wonder how many churches have declined while congratulating themselves? Are we one of them?

Not all death is seen from the outside. We had a parable of that in the two palm trees in front of our church. One was alive; one was dead. In the summer the dead one was covered with a beautiful vine so that outwardly the tree looked alive. But in winter we could see that the tree was dead, for there was no cover-up. We were reluctant to cut it down because the vine was so lovely. But the freeze came and killed the living tree; so both were removed.

Writing in *The Christian Century,* Halford Luccock spoke of a church like this. He called it "The Little Jack Horner Memorial," named after the saint who

". . . stuck in his thumb,

Pulled out a plum,

And said, 'What a good boy am I.' "

Said Luccock: "It is a beautiful church located on Evergreen

Avenue. The spirit of Little Jack Horner hovers over it like a guardian angel. The members repeat in antiphonal chorus, 'What good little boys and girls we are! We're sitting pretty.' At least part of that is true: they are sitting. On the Rock of Ages founded what can shake their sure repose? Apparently nothing. They suffer no attacks of spiritual insomnia. No agony in the heart keeps them from their rest." [2]

Not only had the church at Sardis died, it was even unaware of the fact. Like Samson of old, to them God was lost, power was gone, and they knew it not. When danger threatened, they expected victory but met defeat.

Even so, there is no utter despair. Though John's words were harsh, there was a ray of hope. This is the miraculous thing about the Christian faith: While there is despair over man's beginnings, his sin, there is always hope held out for his future, for his forgiveness. Listen: "Awake, and strengthen what remains and is on the point of death . . . You have still a few names in Sardis, people who have not soiled their garments; and they shall walk with me in white, for they are worthy" (Rev. 3:2–4, RSV).

To those "live Christians" he does not say: "Separate yourselves and come out from among them." Not at all. If the church is dead, keep yourselves alive. If you cannot bring life to the church, find spiritual growth for yourself. Help bring about a change.

I do feel that there are times when a change is profitable for both a church and a person; not just to be changing, not to run away, but because a pattern is set, a mood is established, and if there is to be any growth or development, it is wise for all concerned to make a change.

A friend of mine was a regular attender and contributor to our church. But he was not a member. He just would not move his membership. His wife was a member, but she never came. They talked it over, talked with me, and decided to move to another church and start all over. They did. He became superintendent of the Sunday School and later a deacon, and the entire family was activated. In their case, change was helpful. They came alive.

Even to those "dead ones" there is a word of hope. Death usually means the end of everything. But not to the Christians. The mystery cult of Cybele, which claimed the power of restoring life to the dead, flourished in Sardis. In fact, Cybele was the patron saint of the city. So the writer of Revelation points out that the Christian's real resurrection is to new life. Those dead ones are urged to repent. And repentance means that they are not merely to quit what they are doing; but for them repentance means to put life and reality into their activities.

If the people at Sardis would truly repent, change their minds, change their direction, their ways, their purposes, there is promise and hope for them. Honor and security belong to the faithful Christian.

He is given a white robe, symbolizing purity in contrast to the brightly colored garments of Sardis' revellers. His name may be blotted from the citizenship rolls if he refuses to worship the Emperor, and he may be kept from the voting polls; but his name can never be removed from the Lamb's Book of Life.

NOTES

1. Carlyle Marney, "The Recovery of Courage." Copyright 1963 Christian Century Foundation. Reprinted by permission from the December 1963 issue of *The Pulpit*.

2. Simeon Stylites: "The Twelve Worst Churches." Copyright 1951 Christian Century Foundation. Reprinted by permission from the March 7, 1951 issue of *The Christian Century*.

CHAPTER TEN:

Philadelphia, Opportunities, Not Problems
Revelation 3:7–13

Have you ever considered that it is seemingly easier for most of us to talk about what's wrong than it is about what is right? We can point out the failures of a political party or ways the current administration is messing things up. We can show how some civic club or lodge member lets the club or lodge become a substitute for the church. We can tell how a fraternity or sorority falls short of its charter. We can complain about the hypocrisy of some church member who does not maintain the standards of the high calling of Christ. We can point out the failures of the church.

Maybe you have heard something like this at a gathering: "Well, I'm certainly not going to be the next one to leave. I'm going to be the *last* so you won't talk about me the way you have been talking about so-and-so." (Note the use of *you* instead of *we!*) But the thing is, we cannot always be present in every group to keep them from discussing us. And, let us remember, not all of this dissecting is malicious. Some of it is, but a lot is done in a friendly sort of way.

Can't you imagine that there must have been a lot of squirming when John started writing those letters to the churches. Man, if, as I believe, each of the churches saw all of the letters, what discussions there must have been!

Listen to the self-persecuted people of Pergamum: "Well (with a Jack Benny inflection), it's about time John found out about that bunch of heretics. Why, did you know they received a member without properly baptizing him! They even shared the eucharist with a believer from Sardis. Did you ever?"

Then, old effervescent Ephesus, all thunder and no lightning, took to task the timed, tainted Thyatirans. Poor old Smyrna did not get much of a blast from John, but the other churches must have seethed: "If John were not so old and would get around the district more often, he'd *learn* some things about Smyrna." When it came to Philadelphia, not a word of condemnation from John. Maybe there was no grumbling from the other churches.

Yes, I know what has been said about people not criticizing or persecuting a church because it is not doing anything worth the trouble to criticize or persecute. Some of the people may have talked about Philadelphia, but not John. He had nothing but praise and encouragement for the Christians there.

There is more than one ancient city named Philadelphia. One was in the area of Ephesus and Smyrna. However, I am taking this to be the ancient city that we now know as Amman, Jordan.

Philadelphia as a city dates back many centuries. Because of its fine water supply (another factor a city should consider as it plans for growth) the site attracted settlers as early as 1600 B.C. By the thirteenth century before Christ it was known as Rabbah Ammon, the city of the children of Ammon. It is mentioned in the book of Deuteronomy.

When Alexander the Great's empire was carved up by his generals after his death, Seleucus took Syria and Ptolemy took Egypt. Amman frequently changed hands between these two warring factions. By the third century before Christ the town was captured by Ptolemy Philadelphia, who renamed the city after himself. The name Philadelphia comes from two Greek words meaning "love" and "brother"; hence, "the City of Brotherly Love." It continued to be known as Philadelphia until Islamic times, and the Greek Orthodox Bishop who resides in the present city is called "the Bishop of Petra and Philadelphia."

However, the town's period of greatest prosperity was under the rule of the Romans when Amman was one of the cities of the Decapolis. Well preserved ruins of the magnificent Roman amphitheater, which seated six thousand people, are located in the center of the modern city, just across the street from the Philadelphia Hotel. The city flourished under the Romans because it became an important trade center connecting Rome with access to the Red Sea via the Gulf of Aqaba. You can read Lawrence of Arabia's *Seven Pillars of Wisdom* and learn its value in World War I.

Amman is built, like Rome and San Francisco, upon a series of hills—*jebels*. Today it has experienced a rebirth of its ancient prosperity. It is also a continuing pawn between warring factions: Arabs, Jews, and Al-Fatah. From rags to riches is its modern story. From a small frontier town in 1947 it has grown into a bustling city of over a half million people which serves as the political center of the Hashemite Kingdom of Jordan.

The city's unprecedented growth is reflected in the sharp increase in real estate prices. Land which in 1947 sold for $3.00 per square *are* (about 120 square yards) is now worth nearly $10,000 in the business center of the city and some $5,000 in the suburbs. The present vista of Amman is that of a beautiful terraced city, with gleaming limestone buildings.

Early Philadelphia was called "the Missionary City" because it was the center for the spreading of the Greek language, culture, and manner. So, it could also serve as a center for spreading the Christian faith.

Because the letter is primarily concerned with the church's relationship to the Jews, it opens with the claim that Christ is the true Messiah. So here a door is opened to the Christians to give them an opportunity for the conversion of the Jews, with every expectation of success.

With Smyrna, the Christians of Philadelphia shared the honor of greater fidelity to the gospel than any other of the churches. Philadelphia seems to be the choice city of the seven. Yet, today Christianity is a struggling minority in the city of Amman.

In fact, Christianity is so weak and ineffectual in the area of its origins that this should give us pause. We should take careful looks at ourselves to see whether or not our cities and our churches will be in eclipse in a few generations. It could be, you know.

An open door of opportunity stood before this church because, even though it had little strength, it had kept the faith. This door of opportunity had been opened because the church had been faithful to its past opportunities. No church, or person, will be given larger occasions unless the past and present chances, no matter how small, are well used. Anyway, if we have not done or will not do our present task, how can we expect anything bigger or better to come our way? If we have not accomplished our present task, there is no reason to believe that we will go through larger openings if and when they do come to us. I have seen churches wither and fade because they did not use their present opportunities.

During college days one of my favorite poets was Edna St. Vincent Millay. Particularly her poem "Renascence" impressed me along with "O World, Thou Choosest Not the Better Part." In her poem "The Suicide," she talks about a person who took his own life then in the afterlife stood looking for a new task to perform. After waiting for the assignment that never came, the person asked why not, and the voice of God spoke: "Thou hast had thy task, and laidst it by."

No power, no person could stop the work of the church at Philadelphia. The gates of hell could not prevail, withstand, if the church took this open door of opportunity. It may not be the strongest church in the Decapolis Association, or in the Asia Minor Convention, but it had an opportunity! It may not even be the biggest or best opportunity, but there it was, set before them as an open door.

The phrase "open door" has two meanings. First, it means access to God. There is no hindrance, no barrier between God and man. However, there is a deeper meaning. Paul used the term to mean a possibility for missionary activity in spreading the gospel. Thus, let us say that it has a both/and meaning: Where there is access to God there is missionary opportunity; where there is missionary potential there must be access to God. Each depends upon the other.

There are churches, and people, in life who seem not to have any open doors, or at least they seem to be limited in the work they can do. We need to remember that what may be an opportunity for one is not that for another. As we differ in ability, so we differ in service. For example, there are those who are invalids. Many of them use those sick beds constructively; unfortunately, others are such grouches that they repel people. One dear little lady of three score and six years gave a quiet Christian witness that impressed all those around her. She even thanked the nurses for the shots to relieve the pain.

Anne Woodfin sent me a little note the other day which speaks to this idea: "When I read the following from *Take My Hand* by Wilson, I thought of you and Ann: 'I wonder if you know how much your Christian witness means to others in this hospital—patients, nurses, doctors, all struggling with their human pains and problems. "Think of Mary," I hear over and over, "We think we have troubles, what about her? Yet always trusting, always smiling, never a word of complaint.' " Well, without being too personal, I tell you that Ann Lee has used adversity as an opportunity for the reality of her Christian faith.

There are those who never go any place, or who feel that their place of living and working is too insignificant for great achievements. But, look what William Allen White did for Emporia, Kansas, or Wilfred Grenfell in Labrador, or Guy Howard, "The Walking Preacher of the Ozarks," or Harry Golden, "The Carolina Israelite." There is still truth in the philosophy of building a better mousetrap, even in Christian service.

My soul! what we could do here in New Orleans, America's most interesting city, one of the world's most fabled cities, *if we would!*

To see the needs of people where they are and to meet those needs in the spirit of Christ, that is the greatest of all opportunities and the greatest of achievements.

Keep this in mind: While Christ may open doors before us, he cannot force us to go through them. An expressive little quatrain states the idea:

> You can lead a horse to water,
> But you cannot make him drink.
> You can send a boy to college,
> But you cannot make him think.

I once heard a missionary speak on the idea of the open door of missionary opportunity in China. He closed his message with a prayer. In the prayer was a sentence which has remained etched on my memory through the years: "Lord, Thou hast shown us the open door; give us sense enough to go through it." You see, if we refuse to go through whatever door is open in front of us right now, then we shut the door of future possibilities right in our own face.

The church at Philadelphia was not particularly strong. In fact, the writer says: "I know that you have but little power." They were strong spiritually, but not numerically, socially, or materially. They were lacking in both finances and in trained leadership. Such factors often cause a church to hesitate in tackling a big job. Many churches want to wait until they feel that their ability is equal to any task before they attempt anything. God does not give us opportunities that are beyond our abilities. He does give us strength equal to the task assigned. When it was needed, Pentecostal power was supplied for the Pentecostal task.

Although the church was not strong, another word was said about them which implies some hidden resources: ". . . you have kept my word and have not denied my name."

It is possible to be a close student of the Bible, to know well its contents, and not even be a Christian. It is thoroughly possible to be orthodox in belief and yet be spiritually dead. Ephesus was like that. Yet, the chances are that the one who studies his Bible, knows why he is a Christian, knows what he believes and why, is more apt to be an active Christian than the one who does not.

On this matter of knowing and using the right words but not being true in practice, let me illustrate with a personal experience. Some years ago I was in Washington, D. C. While there, a friend and I went to see the Islamic Center to see the new Mosque that had been built in our nation's capital. After the guide had explained matters to us, there was a lull in the conversation. I spoke to the guide in Arabic, using the few words some Arab friends had taught me. Quick as a flash, he returned the greeting, and with a smile said to the group: "Ah, meet a fellow Moslem." I hastened to assure him that such was not the case, that, on the contrary, I was a minister of the Christian faith. He smiled, and said: "But, you used the right words. You proclaimed your belief in Allah, the one true God, thus we are brothers in the faith." You see, I had used the right words, but I was not a Moslem. Just so, having the right words does not make one a Christian, a follower of Christ.

Evidently, severe persecution had not yet reached Philadelphia. These Christians had endured trials at the hands of their Jewish brethren. The rift between the church and the synagogue was severe. The wealth and power of the Jewish community did nothing to soften feelings toward the poorer Christians. But the Jews were to learn that the Christians were loved of God.

While severe persecution had not come, there is no promise that they will escape. The promise is, rather, that no power can overcome their souls. Even the historian Gibbon in *The Decline and Fall of the Roman Empire* says that among the seven churches of Asia, Philadelphia remained erect, a column in a scene of ruins.[1]

Come with me, now, for a closer look at the promises made to the church at Philadelphia. The promises spoke of a keeping power, a growing likeness, and an increasing usefulness.

"Because you have kept my word . . . I will keep you . . . I will write the name of my God . . . I will make him a pillar in the temple of my God."

Name, of course, stands for character, and to have written upon us the name of God means that we are to share in a growing likeness of God. Just as silver has to meet certain standards before the name "sterling" is stamped upon it, so the standards of keeping the Word means being stamped with the name of God.

The city of Philadelphia had at one time been given a new

name, NEOKAISAREIA—"The New Caesar," in honor of the emperor who had helped rebuild the city after a destructive earthquake. All history has done this, and we are not an exception, not with all of our "Kennedyalia." But this new name for the city had been used for only a short time. (Notice how the writer made use of a common fact of knowledge.) These Christians are assured that although they are citizens of an earthly city, they are also citizens of the New Jerusalem, bearing the name of God in Christ. Although their names could be, and were, removed from the citizenship rolls of Philadelphia, and the city could have its name changed; their names could never be removed from the city of their God.

The conquering Christian is to be made a pillar in the temple of God. Note that the word is *pillar* not *pillow*. A pillar is a stable thing, a means of support, which to those earthquake conscious people meant permanence. A pillar carried with it the idea of steadfastness or constancy. A pillar is always in its place to be depended upon. Thus we speak of so-and-so as being a "pillar of the church." But such a pillar is not one who supports the church on Sunday and lets it go on Monday. He does not support the church at the hour of prayer and then topple it with a shady business deal on Thursday. He does not support the church at home and wreck it when he is away from home in some strange city where no one knows him.

I read the story of an American army officer in the city of Berlin shortly after World War II. Walking down the streets he came upon a bawdy house. On the outside were lewd, suggestive pictures of women making an appeal to the lusts of the flesh. Having been separated from his wife for many months, all the natural impulses of physical desire surged within him. And, believe me, temptation hits us hardest where our impulses are the most natural. But the officer remembered his wife and family in the deep relationships of love. In Berlin, no one would know. *But he would know!* So, he squared his shoulders and walked away, a true pillar of marital fidelity.

Some convention goers here in New Orleans need to remember that when they walk down our Bourbon Street. *And many do!*

One of the distressing things about Vietnam is the distressingly high rate of venereal disease and drug use. What in the name of common sense are we doing to our youth, our future?

A pillar is also an ornament, not just a thing of strength, but also of beauty. Those people knew the classic beauty of Greek architecture. They were familiar with those Doric and Corinthian columns. They knew their beauty as well as their utility. Any modern visitor is likewise impressed with both the durability and the exquisite beauty of those ancient constructions.

There is nothing so beautiful as a good life, or the charm of genuine goodness. The Bible uses the phrase "the beauty of holiness" as an idea of genuine worship. Said the psalmist: "O worship the Lord in the beauty of holiness." Those supporters of the Philadelphia church were fascinating folk—pillars of the church with both beauty and strength.

From the first-century church of Philadelphia there are two things for us of the twentieth-century church to hear: First, there is an open door of opportunity for today's church, really an unprecedented opportunity with modern transportation, communication, and knowledge. Second, he who uses his opportunity in the service of Christ is as secure as a pillar in the temple of God.

NOTES

1. Ray Summers, *Worthy Is the Lamb* (Nashville, Broadman Press, 1951), cf. p. 123.

CHAPTER ELEVEN:

Laodicea, Compromise with Affluence
Revelation 3:14–21

The city of Laodicea stood on the great Roman road which led from Damascus to Arabia. It was about fifty miles from Philadelphia and was the capital of Phrygia. More strategically situated for commerce than for war, Laodicea rose to prominence under the peaceful rule of Rome. It was a banking center and was famous for its textile industry and a medical preparation for the eyes. Laodicea was characterized by riches. Even when it was partially destroyed by an earthquake about A.D. 60, the city needed no help from the Roman government. It did its own rebuilding, for it did not want to be declared a major disaster area subject to urban renewal. We all like that kind of independence.

Laodicea was the major commercial city of the area. Three major Roman roads crisscrossed the city with expressways and interchanges and access roads. It is somewhat natural for such a city to become complacent and lethargic. It had it made! As in the other cities we have discussed, the spirit of the city had carried over into the church.

All of this John knew. Here, as in the other letters, he identifies the church in some measure with the city in which it is located. But in no other is his local knowledge so much in evidence.

This is a church in an affluent society without either a hot enthusiasm or a cold antagonism toward religious matters. Even open hostility would be preferable to this lukewarm, repulsive indifference, for it would at least suggest that religion was something to be in earnest about. Spiritually, the church is said to be poor, blind, and naked, and not all the banks, looms, and pharmacies in the city could provide for its needs.

Early in the first century a church was founded in Laodicea. It may have been that the church was established by Epaphras, whom Paul names in his epistle to the Colossians. Colossae was only seven or eight miles away. Evidently, the church began well and did a good work for a time. Paul mentions the church several times in the Colossian epistle:

> For I want you to know how greatly I strive for you, and for those at Laodicea, . . . rejoicing to see your good order and the firmness of your faith in Christ (Col. 2:1–5, RSV).

> Epaphras, who is one of yourselves, . . . for I bear him witness that he has worked hard for you and for those in Laodicea . . . Give my greetings to the brethren at Laodicea. . . . And when this letter has been read among you, have it read also in the church of the Laodiceans; and see that you read also the letter from Laodicea (Col. 4:12–16, RSV).

But something had gone wrong with the church, because the most stinging rebuke of all is given to them. It is the one church about whom nothing good is said. I think this a bit too harsh. The charge against them, lukewarmness, has become the classic example of what is most disliked in a church or in an individual.

When a person is described as average, he is just as near to the bottom as to the top. So he is neither good nor bad, just average. No doubt, people can remain average all of their lives. Many do. But most are likely to change for the better or for worse. If an average person decides he is going to get out of that classification and try to move nearer to the top, it means he has decided to plan, study, and work and the time devoted to these tasks is not to be curbed by rules or regulations.

The church at Ephesus, you remember, brought upon itself the threat of destruction because its abundant zeal lacked the proper motive. But Laodicea had neither zeal nor motive. "Would that you were either hot or cold." The word 'cold' refers to those who have never been touched by the gospel. Matthew records a similar statement used by Jesus: "He that is not with me is against me" (Matt. 12:30).

This means that one is either hot or cold, for or against Christ. Lukewarmness, tepidity, indifference toward Christ is looked upon as being denial, and/or opposition. It is better, maybe, to be untouched by the flame of Christ than to have smoldering embers, half-choked by ashes. Old fires are often more difficult to rekindle, for they have to be coaxed or fanned.

Had one of us visited the city we would have found it to be progressive and prosperous. A visit to the church would have been impressive, too. The people were well-to-do, had a beautiful choir, and a good preacher. But something would seem to be lacking. One has to be around awhile in order to sense attitudes. This is a good reason for newcomers to get a feel of a church, learn its outlook, and know something of its philosophy of and approach to the Christian faith.

The Laodiceans were not open, flagrant sinners. They were not heretics. They were not antagonistic. But they had lost their interest. Their religion had become a form.

Why is it that here in our own church fewer than one-half of our resident members are present at worship on any given Sunday? This same ratio is true of other churches. In fact, a rule of thumb for building a new sanctuary is to provide seating for 50 percent of the membership.

Why, too, do the national statistics show that more than 20 percent of church members never contribute to the support of their church.

We cannot help but be saddened by the professing Christians who seldom avail themselves of the services of the church for worship. Most are not openly opposed to the church; they are just indifferent which is far worse. This attitude says: Yes, we know what the church stands for and what it has to offer, we really believe in it, but we just don't think it worthwhile. They have neither the courage to openly renounce Christ and the church nor to practice their Christianity. They cannot take their paganism straight, and they are uncomfortable in being Christian.

Of the last four funerals I have conducted, all were for people above seventy years of age. Two of them were members of our church who had not attended in years. The other two had no connection with any church and I went into that very personal situation as a stranger.

Halford Luccock described a modern Laodicea: "This [church] has a long ancestry, going back to earliest times in Asia Minor . . . : It has today a sweet reasonableness, undisturbed by any unruly emotion . . . It is neither hot nor cold . . . In its eyes the highest Christian virtue is languor—not a vulgar, sprawling languor, [horrors no!] but a cultured, refined apathy. A wandering pilgrim who visited the Laodicea Church lately reports that they were singing, strangely enough, 'Onward Christian Soldiers.' When they dragged out the lines,

Onward then, ye people,
Join our happy throng,

he felt that there were three things wrong. They were not a throng; they were not obviously happy; and they did not look as though they cared whether anyone joined them or not." [1]

The complaint at Laodicea was against its lukewarmness. The church was neither hot nor cold. It was in utter indifference. There was no heat of fervent zeal. It was lukewarm, tepid. And few things are more distasteful than tepid tea, coffee, soup, or anything else that is supposed to be hot. Cold vichyssoise or chilled consommé are all right but not if they are lukewarm. It is better to deal with a church that is either frozen or blazing than with one that is tepid, lukewarm. (Remember my Yale classmate, Jason Shirah, who preferred trying to restrain the fanatics of the South to raising the dead in New England.)

Let me submit three things that are bothersome about lukewarmness.

For one thing, the lukewarm is the hardest to reach, be this a person or a group, for anything. An open opponent is easier to convert than one who just doesn't care.

Second, indifference strikes a blow to usefulness. It causes us to only half try. It tends to paralyze. Such a lack of interest robs of charm. For example, is anything less charming than a flabby handshake? During one of our recent gubernatorial campaigns I was asked to pray at the occasion. (I preferred praying for the state!) At this meeting I met one of our leading Louisiana-Washington lawmakers. I had always thought rather well of him, but never have I felt a clammier, flabbier handshake! Now I wonder if he is just as flabby as a lawmaker. And, looking at his record, he has *never* submitted a significant piece of legislation in his more than two decades of being a public servant!

How many of us buy from the salesman who says: "You don't want to buy nothin,' do you?" And it's not just the terribly poor English, although that should be enough to ruin the sale and is inexcusable. (A cigarette does rather well with its poor English grammar advertising.) Instead, it is the indifferent, don't-care attitude.

In the third place, lukewarmness in a Christian most grossly misrepresents Christ. We could never say that Jesus Christ was indifferent about his task. And a Christian is supposed to represent Christ. In fact, Christian means "a little Christ."

In the Old Testament there is a reference which describes what I am saying: "Ephraim is a cake not turned" (Hos. 7:8, RSV). This is just a polite way of saying, "You guys are half-baked!" This is a humorous, though stern, rebuke. The picture is of a cake burned on one side and raw on the other; therefore, useless. The sin of halfheartedness is not new, and few there are who escape it.

There are, unfortunately, those who are Christian in name yet who care not to part from the world. Their business habits are a compromise of trying to serve both God and mammon. In social and domestic life they try to relish the treasure of religion amidst unchristian pursuits. They have enough Christianity to feel uncomfortable in doing wrong, but not enough to feel comfortable in doing right.

The following illustration may be a bit extreme, but it does point out the dangerous evil of trying to play both sides, even in innocence.

Wong Lung, the principal character in Pearl Buck's novel *The Good Earth* had provided a good home for his uncle for many years, not out of love for his uncle but because of family loyalty.

When the uncle proved responsible for the moral downfall of Wong's son, Wong resolved to expel the uncle from his home. "Drive me out, if you dare," said the uncle, opening his coat to reveal in the lining the badge of a notorious band of robbers that had been kidnapping the women of the community and burning the farmer's homes. Then Wong understood why his family and house had never been molested. He had been safe so long as he fed his uncle's household. Wong said no more about his uncle's leaving.

So often it is that sin and corruption gain strangleholds even on those who would do good.

How many people there are who are like Wong. Perhaps each of us to some extent. How many of us do what we know to be wrong, or refrain from challenging wrong in others, because there is fear that we may suffer personally or incur some wrath on our loved ones? Too many of us wish to retain our status at the expense of moral Christian principles.

But, we cannot "run with both the hare and the hounds." Spiritually we are the one thing or the other. As Paul put it in one of my favorite passages: "Be not conformed to [the things of] this world, but be transformed by the renewing of your mind" (Rom. 12:2).

Now, let's take a look at what was said to the church at Laodicea. "Be zealous and repent!" In other words, "Get hot!" How can lukewarm water be brought to a boil? By applying heat, of course. Here are three suggestions as to how to apply heat to Laodicea, and to ourselves.

First, the Laodiceans needed to face facts about themselves. So do we. They needed to see themselves as they were: disgustingly satisfied with themselves. And they didn't have too much to be proud of at that. Do we ever? It was when the prodigal son faced the facts about himself that he came to himself and turned toward home.

In the second place, they needed to see themselves as they might become. They did not need to stay as they were. In place of spiritual poverty they could have riches, for God's storehouse is abundantly full. In place of nakedness they could have spotless garments. Instead of blindness they could have sight.

Five years ago we had five self-study committees taking a

look at five areas of our church: worship, education, evangelism, missions, and stewardship. Those committees projected definitions, purposes, objectives, and specific recommendations in written reports. Out of that came a charted course which we have been following. Some of the things were done, many were left undone.

Right now we are in the midst of a "self inventory," trying to take a look at ourselves to see what kind of people we are and the kind of things we want for our church. The questionnaires will be tabulated and evaluated as we try to project a course for us to follow in the critical days of the seventies.

The third thing was to let Christ enter their lives and their church. We shall say more about this later.

There were three chief businesses of the city. Each is used to illustrate both the present attitudes and the future possibilities of the church.

First, Laodicea was a banking center. While the city had material wealth, the church was spiritually impoverished—just the opposite of Smyrna. A man can possess all the money in the world and yet be poor in what makes life worthwhile. Would that some of my younger and older friends could see that. I could illustrate with example after example of men who say that they wish they had learned sooner that money isn't everything. And I could also illustrate with those who still seem to think that it is. They feel that if they can't take it with them, then they just aren't going. My, what some members of our church could do with their money right now and even more with some sort of a legacy instead of allowing so much to go for taxes.

Second, it was a black wool market center. (Not the center for a black market in wool futures, although some of that probably went on, too.) They produced a glossy black wool which made the finest of garments. In spite of this they were spiritually naked. Their robes of haughty self-sufficiency did not cover them before the Lord. Fine clothes, and I like them as much as anyone, may help make the man, but a man needs the robes of righteousness even more.

Third, it was a medical-pharmaceutical center. They made an ointment for the eyes. Travelers coming in off the hot, sandy, windblown desert roads found this first-century "Murine" that got the red out a welcome relief. But they were spiritually blind. They needed their eyes open. And only Christ could give them a salve to cure that blindness.

The church at Laodicea had everything but Christ; and he was trying to get in. But Christ never forces entrance. "Behold, I stand at the door and knock; if any one hears my voice and opens the door, I will come in" (Rev. 3:20, RSV). To Laodicea, as an example of failure, Christ is identified as the one incapable of failure.

Lest the severity of the rebuke leave them utterly despondent, thinking themselves abandoned by Christ, they are told that they are rebuked in order that by repentance they might find forgiveness. Some people seemingly have to be dealt with severely and roughly in order to induce repentance. So these Laodiceans still have a chance to repent and change. This gospel of the second chance is the marvelous miracle of the Christian faith.

At Philadelphia Christ was showing an open door of opportunity. In Laodicea he is confronted with a closed door and he is seeking admission.

St. Paul's Cathedral in London has Holman Hunt's original painting of this unforgettable portrait of Christ standing at a closed door seeking entrance. As you know, the artist deliberately left off an outside latch, for this door can be opened only from the inside. There is a poignant sadness one feels as he stands in front of this beautiful painting and watches people go by and give but a passing glance to this seeking Christ.

Christ is still on the same mission which brought him into the world. The first move toward salvation—yours, mine, the Laodiceans—is made by Christ. He seeks us before we seek him. He does all that is within his power. He knocks at the door, and that is all he can do. He never enters where he is not welcome. He never crashes or barges in. If we do not open to receive him, he does not enter.

When God set in motion the creative process, what he intended to produce was Christ and men like Christ who respond in faith and obedience. Wherever he is present, God's creative and recreative power is at work. It is this Christ who addresses the Laodiceans, summoning them to find their true wealth in the recreating love of God. The very harshness of the censure is proof of a love that is satisfied only with the best.

Christ asserts his love for the Laodiceans as a whole. He loves them all, not just the faithful but the unfaithful as well. He does not chasten in anger but in love. The chastening is to produce repentance. If Christ is become our guest of life, then we must let him in.

NOTES

1. Simeon Stylites: "The Twelve Worst Churches." Copyright 1951 Christian Century Foundation. Reprinted by permission from the March 7, 1951 issue of *The Christian Century*.

CHAPTER TWELVE:

Antioch, The Church Comes of Age

It was a memorable event in the history of man when the name Christian was first given to the followers of Jesus Christ. Hitherto, they had called themselves disciples, brethren, followers of the Way, Nazarenes, and Galileans.

We have often heard it said that the name Christian was given in derision and ridicule. The record does not indicate that such was the case. Rather, those people were so patterning their lives after the one they believed and whose teachings they practiced that the Gentile world identified them with their leader. A perfectly natural thing to do.

Dietrich Bonhoeffer, the martyred young German theologian of World War II, is credited with the phrase, "the church has come of age," meaning that the church has grown up so that it must meet the issues of the day in a mature way. This is what happened at Antioch.

Antioch was the chief city of the Hellenic East. It was next to Alexandria in importance. It was an intellectual, cultural, and commercial center easily in reach of the major cities of Cappadocia, Syria, and Arabia. Antioch was much like our major cities of the twentieth century: rich, sophisticated, and elegant.

A thing that captures our imagination is that the procedure of establishing Christianity was to capture the cities for Christ. As go the cities, so goes the country. The city is the center from which radiate the forces that build up or tear down a civilization. Surely, the cities are the most serious and difficult problem confronting Christianity today. What to do with our secular urbanization? our high-rise apartments, with their depersonalized, impersonal living? our slums, with their breeding place of crime and all that goes with a metropolitan area? But from the beginning, Christianity took on the city problem *first* and was successful.

In the United States we have spent so much time in the rural areas, especially we Baptists, that we do not know what to do in the city. We are no longer a rural people, not with some 85 percent of our population in urban areas. We are no longer a rural denomination, even if we do have more rural churches. Our rural roots do not transplant very easily in the "concrete jungle." But we must adapt to this new environment and find new plantings of our faith. These early churches of the New Testament give us good clues.

The record says that men from Cyrene and Cyprus went to Antioch and preached to the Grecians there, and some of them believed and accepted Christ. An earlier account in the second chapter of Acts records the events of Pentecost. On that day, men from Cyrene, Cyprus, Cappadocia, and Arabia were present. Their experience at Pentecost fitted them to carry the gospel back to their homes. And, remember how closely Antioch was associated with those places.

There are two significant facts for us to consider. First, those men from Cyrene and Cyprus had experiences which fitted them to carry the gospel with them. In other words, they could be Christian wherever they were, at home or abroad. And sometimes it is easier to be a Christian at home than it is away. This applies to businessmen who travel, men in military service, persons on vacation, or students away at college. At Pentecost, those men had a vital, life-changing experience that gave them something to take home or to take abroad.

What are the thousands of people who come to New Orleans —"The Gateway of the Americas," "America's Most Interesting City"—finding out about Christ from us? Thousands of students come here every year, and hundreds of international visitors pass through here. Is there any Pentecost they can take with them?

On the whole they can find a great deal, if they want to and will, and many of them have. For example, the influence of this one church is scattered everywhere because of such people in the past, students and others. Businessmen, doctors, other professional people, teachers, pastors, musicians, and missionaries are all over the world who found some kind of a Pentecostal experience here. And this is still happening.

But sometimes these who come to us do not learn the right things. Sometimes inconsiderate words are spoken to them about their religion or racial backgrounds which send them away with bad opinions and feelings. You see, our responsibility is twofold: Our witness to Christ must be sure and effective, and we are to take our Christian witness with us everywhere.

In the second place, to be driven from one place to another because of persecution does not mean the collapse of Christianity nor the forestalling of the gospel. Just because missionaries were forced out of China some two decades ago does not mean that Christianity has been blotted out there. Only those Christians with blonde hair and blue eyes left; those with black hair and slanted black eyes remain. There is evidence of Christian activity in China today. Some Christians there are steadfast in their beliefs and aggressive in their preaching.

One other thing: When missionaries were forced out of China, at least in so far as Southern Baptists are concerned, it meant that new fields of opportunity were opened. Those scattered missionaries went to Taiwan, Thailand, Malasia, and Indonesia. To be scattered abroad means a new method of extending and expanding the gospel, if we will be faithful in our Christian witness.

There are three things that stand out in the development of this group of Christians at Antioch that are marks of distinction for any church. With them a church is effective; without them a church withers away. These three factors are evangelism, missions, and benevolent stewardship. Nothing new, but something startling when practiced, even today.

First, consider evangelism. The Antioch church refused the bondage of the traditional, literal, legalistic Judaism of the Jerusalem church. Jerusalem insisted on such a thing as circumcision of all converts. So a delegation went from Antioch to Jerusalem for a "doctrinal council." They did not go hat-in-hand; they went as autonomous equals. The result was the establishment of a basic New Testament principle: "Salvation is by the grace of God through faith in Jesus Christ alone." No external, man-made rites, be they circumcision, baptism, creedal pledges, or sacraments are necessary. Thus, Antioch was freed to proclaim the gospel of repentance and faith, *and they did!*

Evangelism changed the morals of the city of Antioch. Evangelism changed the center of Christian influence to Antioch. Ten church councils met there between the years 252–380 A.D., and Antioch was the leading patriarch of the early church.

We must realize that there are many forms of evangelism. We cannot say that if one church does not follow the procedures and methods of another church that one or the other is not evangelistic. Evangelism is presenting the claims of Christ and pressing for a decision in Christ's favor no matter how it is done. Any church that ceases to be evangelistic soon withers.

And there is abundant evidence in our day that evangelism is being curtailed.

No one can say that our own church is not evangelistic; neither can we say that we are doing an adequate job of presenting the claims of Christ. We are doing some, but certainly not enough. And this is especially true in our person-to-person relationships.

One thing stands out in the evangelism at Antioch: it was done largely by laymen. Laymen began the work and they continued it. There should be no clergy-laity distinctions. The only difference is in degree, not in kind. A moment's reflection shows us that modern communism, for example, has not been spread by "professionals," but by agitated, dedicated laymen, guided by the professionals.

A second factor in the growth of Antioch was its missionary emphasis. When Saul of Tarsus was converted, he was told that he was to carry the gospel to the Gentile world. Now the time had come for Saul to do his work. As the leaders in Antioch sought the will of God, this is what the Holy Spirit revealed: "Set apart for me Barnabas and Saul for the work to which I have called them. Then after fasting and praying they laid their hands on them and sent them off."

Thus the great missionary enterprise was launched which was to carry the gospel across the Roman Empire, and which in three hundred years was to be declared the official religion of that Empire. While Jerusalem was sending out investigating committees, Antioch was sending out missionaries.

Today's obstacles, great as they are, cannot compare with those faced by Antioch. Our numbers are greater, our resources are greater, and our means are more effective. Our "orders" and our "message" are the same as Antioch's.

Some of our modern "guardians of orthodoxy" ought to bear

this in mind. If a church, or a person, is to be disciplined, let it be on matters that count. There is no defense whatsoever for heresy against the gospel. Often, however, heresy against the church is in favor of the gospel. There are those churches who give nothing to further the gospel in the cause of missions. Is there ever any discipline there? Why not? So long as a church is evangelistic and missionary, we have little to fear about its orthodoxy or that it is within the will of God.

The third thing that distinguished the attitude of the Antioch church was its spirit of benevolent stewardship. Not only were they willing to share their spiritual blessings, they shared their material possessions as well, even with Jerusalem.

Unlike Jerusalem, which shared all things in common with each other, Antioch apportioned to everyone according to ability and took an offering every week. Antioch was not a rich church. The same famine was hitting them that was plaguing everyone else. But they were the first body of Christians to attempt to relieve the distress of fellow Christians outside their membership.

These two things accompany each other in a dynamic church, and it is often hard to get the two in proper proportion. A church that keeps its possessions to itself, either spiritual or material, is in danger. It is when both are shared that a church functions properly.

Now, let's go back to where we began: The distinctive name that was given to this group at Antioch—*Christians!* The name did not stand for a political party, like Herodianism. It did not stand for a philosophical school, such as Aristolelians. It stood for the followers of Christ. To deserve the name Christian, if it can ever be deserved, means that the spirit of Christ must permeate us and our thoughts and actions so that we give evidence of a peculiar Christian quality.